CANNABIS ACTIVIST'S HANDBOOK

I0421323

by

Vince McLeod

Also by VJM Publishing:

The Verity Key

Learn Spanish Vocabulary With Mnemonics

Stop Smoking Cigarettes with the Token Economy Method

Table of Contents

INTRODUCTION...

PART ONE: THE FOUR STEPS............................
    1. CORE VALUES..
    2. MEMBERSHIP..
    3. FUNDRAISING...
    4. MEDIA...

PART TWO: A DISCUSSION OF CANNABIS
LAW REFORM RELATED ARGUMENTS.............
    1. ARGUMENTS FOR CANNABIS LAW
    REFORM..
    2. COUNTERING ARGUMENTS AGAINST
    CANNABIS LAW REFORM..............................

PART THREE: TAKING IT TO THE TRENCHES..
    1. AN EXAMPLE PARTY POLICY....................
    2. RUNNING A CAMPAIGN..............................
    3. MISCELLANEOUS...

INTRODUCTION

Like many people, my favourite cannabis story comes from Amsterdam. One summer afternoon I sat on the grass of the Rembrantplein, a two-skin joint in hand, merrily partaking with a couple of friends. I noticed, approaching our group along the side of the square, a uniformed policeman. He came closer. Our eyes met. Under his piercing gaze I exhaled a billowing cloud of White Widow smoke.

And that's it. That's the whole story. The policeman walked on, I took another toke and passed the joint to my friend.

For anyone familiar with Amsterdam this is neither a surprising nor an uncommon story. But for almost every other cannabis user in almost every other part of the world it is remarkable. The actions I carried out, although they harmed no-one, would have resulted in at least arrest and probably a trial and a criminal conviction had I performed them in countless other places supposedly ruled by justice and human dignity.

This handbook is for any individual interested in working towards cannabis law reform. It is for anyone who believes that the freedom I experienced that day in a tiny corner of Northern Europe was not the result of a legal aberration but an inviolable human right. The truth of life as a citizen in any political system is that you have only those rights that you fight for. The Dutch have fought for theirs; we can fight for ours.

There are three parts to this handbook. The first is a detailed examination of the necessary steps and considerations in founding and aiding a cannabis law reform movement. The second is a discussion of the arguments for and against cannabis prohibition from the perspective of a cannabis law reform activist seeking to increase support for repealing prohibition. The third looks at how to take the fight to the public, including a list of example policy points that a cannabis law reform movement or party might promote (movement and party are usually used interchangeably in this book).

Because the practical reality of working towards cannabis law reform is that any efforts will be dependent on individual personalities and local conditions, the information in this handbook is not presented as a set of rules to follow. It is merely an invitation to consider the issues, problems and hurdles that will be faced so that any activist can decide which action is most appropriate for them and for the movement in that time and place.

The freedoms of Amsterdam are not the result of a fluke of legal and cultural coincidence. They represent the vanguard of a movement towards higher principles of justice, a movement that is fated to succeed as humanity continues to defeat the inertia inherited from the barbarism of the past. Cannabis prohibition will be repealed across the world, and it will take its place amongst apartheid, child labour, racial segregation and the criminalisation of homosexuality as an idiocy that must never be repeated. All that stands between us and that point is action taken by cannabis law reform activists.

PART ONE: THE FOUR STEPS

There are four steps to creating a cannabis law reform movement that has a chance of making a difference. The first part of this handbook is divided into four sections, each of which examines one of these steps.

The first of these is for the founding members of the movement to decide what they wish the core values of it to be. There are many considerations that must be weighed before a set of core values can be established, and the first section of this part deals with those.

The second step is for the movement to create a membership and to organise this into some kind of structure. There are a lot of tasks here, and as a consequence the section discussing them is fairly lengthy. It covers everything from the recruitment of new members to the different levels of organisation that a national movement must have.

The third step is to raise funds so that the movement can fight more effectively. Fundraising is mostly a mix of merchandising and soliciting donations, and both of these are discussed in detail, as is the effect of money on party operations.

The fourth step is to learn to fight in the media. The description of how to do this overlaps to some degree with the second part of this handbook, because media coverage is ultimately nothing more than an opportunity to put forward arguments for cannabis law reform.

1. CORE VALUES

Before a cannabis law reform movement can even attract other members, a core of potential members must at least formulate a set of values that they agree on and which can be used as a platform for determining future strategy. The most obvious first value is to facilitate the legalisation of cannabis within a certain legal territory.

Even with this minimal value established, there are likely to be ideological disagreements if the group is sufficiently large. The tendency of ideological disagreements is to factionalise, which can be dangerous for the overall effectiveness of the movement. A set of core values must be strong enough to inspire solidarity between members. If a member is confident that other members hold the same values they will be more inclined to work towards the goals of the movement.

The core values that a cannabis law reform movement adopts will depend on a wide range of factors, from the personalities of the individuals involved to the realities of the political system in which the movement operates. The purpose of this section is to describe the disagreements that will likely arise in this regard and some considerations that must be acknowledged.

The Legalisation Spectrum

One of the first arguments that will occur within a cannabis law reform movement is how far the process of legalisation should go, and how far the movement ought to suggest that it go. Firstly, people might disagree on, for example, whether decriminalisation or outright legalisation is the best solution according to their own values. Secondly, some might calculate that although a certain position is morally desirable it is not practical for the movement to publicly agitate for it. For example, some might personally believe that outright legalisation is the best possibility, but calculate that it would be hard to get the necessary political support for this position to influence law.

Starting from the status quo (assuming this is cannabis prohibition) and moving out towards greater freedom, one passes through deprioritisation, depenalisation, decriminalisation, partial legalisation (of which there are many forms) and total legalisation.

Deprioritisation involves no change in either the legal status of cannabis or the penalties associated with it. It relies on a promise by the police that certain cannabis offences will be given the lowest level of importance, should a police officer have multiple tasks in one time period. It is hard to say if this is necessarily a move away from the status quo, because many police jurisdictions have de facto deprioritisation for simple logistical reasons. This is a very small change and most supporters of cannabis law reform will sneer at it for that reason.

Depenalisation involves no change in the legal status of cannabis, but a decrease in the penalties associated with it. If cannabis possession is punishable with a penal sentence, the maximum severity of the sentence might be reduced. The major advantage with depenalisation is that it involves the smallest move away from the status

8

quo, and could therefore be expected to encounter the least resistance. The major disadvantage is that it offers little or no improvement for those affected by cannabis prohibition, and for this reason it does little to inspire activists.

Decriminalisation involves a change in the legal status for some or all cannabis crimes. Crimes that are currently punished with criminal convictions become civil offences punishable by fines. Under this system, cannabis offences would occupy roughly the same legal status as parking offences. This position has a lot of advantages, the major one being that it offers a significant change in legal consequences for a relatively small change in the status quo.

It should be noted here that many experienced cannabis law reform activists are virulently against the previous three options for the reason that achieving either of them may make it far more difficult to go any further. Firstly, the establishment may believe it has acquiesced on the cannabis issue and that no further negotiation need be entertained. Secondly, many cannabis law reform activists might leave the movement at this point in the false belief that cannabis freedom has been achieved.

Partial legalisation and partial prohibition are the same thing, but an activist might use either term depending on the perspective they are coming from. This might refer to complete freedom to possess and use cannabis, and some freedoms regarding its sale and cultivation. A person might have the freedom to grow a limited number of plants and to deal socially to their friends, but may not have the freedom to set up commercial operations.

The major advantages and disadvantages of this system depend on how involved people are with cannabis culture.

Total legalisation is almost, but not quite, a free-for-all. People would be free to possess, use, grow and sell cannabis in whatever manner they wanted (except in special cases, such as sale to minors). Even within this position there is room for movement: some might advocate for cannabis to be completely legal save for laws that relate to general commercial practice, such as the levying of goods and services taxes. Some might wish for even more freedom than this. The advantage of total legalisation is that it maximises freedom; the major disadvantage is that a position this extreme will meet considerable resistance from both within and outside of the movement.

Ultimately the movement needs to decide what it will be fighting for, who it will be fighting for and what (if anything) could be negotiated. In practice it is extremely unlikely that the movement will ever be in a position to dictate the legislation. Some negotiation will inevitably be involved when legislation is changed.

Experience shows that the balance of opinion within the movement usually falls somewhere around the partial legalisation area of the spectrum, although this will of course depend on local conditions.

Cannabis Taxation

Another early argument will be what level of taxation, if any, should be levied on cannabis if a change in its legal status was made. On this question people will form an opinion on a spectrum from no taxation to high taxation, such as a "vice tax." Again, some people will have a personal preference that differs from what they believe the party should promote. In every cannabis law reform movement there will be those who are hardline ideologues and those who are more interested in finding a compromise with the wider public. A popular compromise is to say that cannabis products will be subject to goods and services or sales taxes.

It might seem silly for the party to argue over what is really a victory condition, but people will argue, and as long as they do it is hard to make forward progress. Ultimately the party must find a balance. The lower the levels of taxation, the more freedom people will have regarding the purchase and use of cannabis. The higher the levels of taxation, the stronger the argument will be for cannabis law reform improving society.

Harm Reduction

Adopting the value of harm reduction is an excellent way of gaining support for the movement. Cannabis prohibitionists have a number of reasons for resisting cannabis law reform, and one of the most significant of these is the belief that cannabis legalisation will cause more harm to both individuals and society. If harm reduction is adopted as a core value, it can help to organise the movement, because future policy and arguments for cannabis law reform can be made with a view to achieving this. It also puts the onus on the opponents of cannabis law reform to prove their case that cannabis prohibition is less harmful than legalisation.

The best thing about putting forward the argument for cannabis law reform under an umbrella of harm reduction is that few people will admit to wanting a policy that leads to more harm. This means that if you can demonstrate conclusively that a certain policy is less harmful, even the prohibitionists will have to concede that it has merit.

The reality is that most discussions on the subject of cannabis law reform ultimately come down to harm reduction, whether the harm in question is inflicted on individuals or on society. To persuade a person to become a supporter of cannabis law reform they must be persuaded that reform would be less harmful to them than the status quo, or would be less harmful to society than the status quo, or both. This point is expanded upon in Part Two.

The Single Issue Question

Few debates have more potential to tear a cannabis law reform movement apart than the question of whether it is to be a "single issue" movement or one that agitates in a number of areas. The potential for danger lies in the fact that there are strong arguments for each side.

In favour of the movement contesting the single issue of cannabis there are the arguments of simplicity and believability. Fighting for cannabis law reform and nothing else means that the movement will attract people for whom reform is the highest priority. It will minimise factionalisation because there will be no reason for members to argue over other issues and the relative importance of those issues. It will ensure that the message is not watered down and that members promoting it are not sidetracked by other issues. A cannabis law reform party that only focuses on cannabis also has the advantage of being more credible. Its members need not claim to have expert knowledge on other policy areas, and will avoid the possibility of looking foolish if challenged on party policy in these areas.

In favour of the movement contesting other issues there are two major arguments. Firstly, if another party is also offering cannabis law reform there is little room in the political system for a cannabis-only party; a voter could get what they wanted, plus more, by voting for someone else. Secondly, even if voters have no other option for cannabis law reform they might easily decide that, on balance, the cannabis issue alone does not weigh heavier than the other issues. Related to this point is the fact that if an activist's argument for cannabis law reform does not sway a voter there is little else that could entice them.

From a pragmatic point of view, it might be a good idea to start the movement around a single issue and then expand into other areas once it has attracted sufficient personnel. This will have the benefit of first establishing party authority on the cannabis issue and then attracting voters who might still be on the fence.

Whether or not the movement adopts one issue or several, it should always be kept in mind that changing position on this question will, at least initially, cost the movement support and will require some restructuring. For this reason it is important for the movement to change position rarely and only if benefits to doing so are clear.

Identification With Cannabis Culture

The movement might have to decide to what extent, if any, it will identify with wider cannabis culture. Although it does not have to make a hard decision on questions such as support for Rastafarianism, it will, to some extent and at least informally, act as an important institution of the cannabis culture in the territory it represents.

Probably the only important decision that needs to be made in this regard is the choice of the party colours. Although red, green and yellow appear to many to be the obvious and logical choice for the colours of a cannabis law reform movement, some will prefer to disassociate themselves from this and will argue for something more "neutral." In practice, one of the greatest challenges the movement will face is recruiting people to the cause, and because red, green and yellow in combination is so widespread in cannabis culture, most cannabis users will recognise it immediately.

Other decisions are not necessarily as important but must be considered. Some may wish to choose Bob Marley as the background music for the party's electoral videos. This will have the benefit of unambiguously declaring what the party stands for but may result in it not being taken as seriously as its members wish it to be.

Even if it declares itself a champion of the wider cannabis culture, the movement ought to avoid adopting elements of the culture that might alienate others. Littering party policy documents with Jamaican patois will turn away far more people than it will attract.

Drugs Other than Cannabis

Many people who have an interest in cannabis law reform will also have an interest in the legal status of other drugs, in particular the psychedelics such as LSD and psilocybin. While many of the humanitarian arguments put forward in favour of cannabis law reform are equally applicable to psychedelics, the nature of the battle to legalise psychedelics is very different.

In particular, there are far more people who use and who have used cannabis than who use and have used psychedelics, and these people have generally used cannabis on a much higher number of occasions and over a longer period. A cannabis law reform activist can count on the fact that there are large numbers of people whose personal experience with cannabis suggests that it should be legal; this cannot be done with the psychedelics. There is also the fact that cannabis has considerable economic potential in hemp form, and no such parallel exists for the psychedelics.

A final, more cynical point is that an examination of the legal penalties for possessing and distributing psychedelics, in comparison to the penalties for cannabis, suggests that anyone attempting to legalise them will meet massive resistance. In some jurisdictions the maximum penalty for supplying psychedelics is on the same scale as for murder.

To agitate for the legalisation of drugs other than cannabis will almost certainly weaken the position of a cannabis law reform activist. They will become vulnerable to the accusation that they wish to legalise drugs that have horrific social consequences, and will be painted as irresponsible and foolish for this reason.

Ancillary Values

A cannabis law reform movement may find common ground with regard to cannabis law reform, but the individual members of the movement will come to it with different perspectives and with different values. The beauty - and the danger - of cannabis law reform is that it crosses most of the political spectrum, from those solely concerned with what is best for society and those solely concerned with what is best for themselves. For this reason, the greater the number of core values the movement adopts the easier it will become to both attract support and attract opposition. Cannabis law reform activists are of any age, either gender, and of any race and class, and because of this it is both possible and desirable to build a movement that spans these divisions.

Adopting the right values from the start is vital because this will form the basis of all future attempts to attract members and to encourage support.

Many activists will approach the issue from the perspective of what is best for society. If they do, chances are good that they have personal values that reflect a centre-left approach. Other activists will be more concerned with what is best for the individual. If they do, they might have personal values that reflect a centre-right approach.

Because cannabis law reform attracts support from across the political spectrum, each potential core value has to be examined with a view to who it will attract and who it will reject. Proclaiming a commitment to truth, freedom and justice is a good idea because few will openly disagree with such values. Equality is trickier, because it might not appeal to people on the right. Personal responsibility is also tricky because it might not appeal to people on the left.

Some values will appeal to those on a certain position on the political spectrum, but will not turn others away. A commitment to reducing unnecessary government interference and waste will appeal more strongly to those on the right, but few on the left will object (although they might then become suspicious that the cannabis law reform movement is a trojan horse for other right-wing values).

Because everyone has their own agenda it might be simpler to decide, from the very beginning, that the movement will only be concerned with cannabis law reform. Doing this will bring the benefit of reducing bickering and factionalisation.

Left-Wing, Right-Wing or Centre?

Many of the potential ancillary values that a cannabis law reform movement could adopt would have the effect of pinning it to a point on the political spectrum.

Because this is so important in the minds of so many people, it might be simpler for the movement to decide whether it is left-wing, right-wing or centrist, so each of these options will be looked at in turn. If the movement does make this decision and commits to a position, the choice to reject or accept most values will be obvious.

First, if a party decides it is left-wing, it would focus on taking votes from social democrats and from environmentalist parties. A left-wing policy might be easier to sell to potential supporters because cannabis users tend to be young and poor, and cannabis users who are neither are much more likely to escape the effects of prohibition anyway (and will, therefore, not consider the issue to be important to them). If the party intends to argue that the savings from the repeal of prohibition would allow more funding for social programs, this might be the best choice. This might also be the best choice if the party decides to focus its efforts on the social harm done by cannabis prohibition.

Second, if a party decides it is right-wing, it would focus on taking votes from libertarians. There is potential to take votes from conservatives, but given that conservative parties have historically fought the hardest against cannabis law reform and that conservative individuals are much less likely to support reform, this might be unlikely. If the party intends to argue that the savings from the repeal of prohibition could be passed back to people in the form of tax cuts, this might be the best choice. This might also be the best choice if the party focuses its efforts on the economic harm done by prohibition.

Third, if a party decides it is centrist, it would take votes from wherever it could get them. Social democrats, environmentalists and libertarians could all find something agreeable in party policy. Regarding the savings from the repeal of prohibition, a centrist party would offer the choice between social programs or tax cuts. Likewise, it could credibly argue against both the social and economic disadvantages of cannabis prohibition.

The choice to target the centre of the political spectrum offers three major advantages. First, agreement on a centrist position will make it easier for the party to counter extremist elements within its ranks, whether these extremists be left-wing or right-wing. Second, a centrist position also gives the party more room for manoeuvrability should political or cultural conditions change. Third, a centrist party is much more likely to find itself in a strong negotiating position post-election. It can play the centre-left and centre-right off against each other and agree to support whichever of the two can offer it the most.

The Nature of a Representative Democracy

This handbook is a guide for cannabis law reform activism, but it is specific to representative democracies. The defining characteristic of representative democracies is that a limited number of elected officials speak for and determine legislation on behalf of the people they represent (at least in theory).

For a cannabis law reform movement to decide how its efforts are best spent, it must first determine who it claims to represent. The obvious answer is that it represents people adversely affected by cannabis prohibition, but because an argument can be made that cannabis prohibition harms everyone, this is not useful. At a minimum, the movement represents cannabis users. In some countries cannabis users will be so numerous that a party could get into power from votes from them alone.

The movement might also decide that it represents people who might directly benefit from cannabis law reform, whether these people are current users or not. Because cannabis has considerable medicinal potential, the movement can claim to also represent sick or elderly people who could benefit from using cannabis but do not for fear of legal repercussions.

If a movement defines who it represents it will be able to target these people much more effectively. A pragmatic solution might be to decide that the movement represents those who would benefit the most from cannabis law reform. The movement must be wary against moves to target other groups of voters due to frustration with trying to gain support from cannabis users. A cannabis law reform movement must always be aware that cannabis users, regardless of their voting habits, are the core constituency. Focusing efforts on getting supporters to vote is far better than attempting to turn neutrals into supporters and then getting them to vote.

Alliances

A cannabis law reform party probably will not exist for long before the question of potential alliances is brought up. The more difficult it is to get enough votes to achieve representation, the stronger people will argue the case of forming an alliance with one or more other parties. If the cannabis law reform party is large it may not need to consider an alliance, and if it is small there are two different kinds of alliance that may be proposed.

The first type is an alliance with a party that already has representation, or is expected to after the next election. The advantage of this is that the cannabis law reform party would theoretically gain immediate representation in the legislative body, or at least a stake in it. The disadvantage is, of course, that after an alliance is formed the cannabis law reform party is dependent on the goodwill of their alliance partner. If the alliance partner chose to ignore or deprioritise cannabis law reform, the cannabis law reform party would have little recourse beyond cancelling the alliance and reforming.

The second type is an alliance with one or several parties that do not have representation, with the plan being that their combined resources would be enough to get it. The advantage here is that the cannabis law reform party has a much better chance at getting representation, and will be able to do so on much better terms if the alliance partners are roughly the same size. The disadvantages are that cobbling together an alliance with a number of smaller parties might be more complicated, and that if any of the alliance parties are extremists who turn voters away, the reputation of the cannabis law reform party could be damaged.

There is a third type, which is more of a pseudo-alliance. It occurs when the cannabis law reform party comes to believe that another party offers a better bet for cannabis law reform than the cannabis law reform party itself, and effectively disbands or does not contest the election. Doing this has the potential to cripple the entire cannabis law reform movement. The most obvious reason for this is that there is little or nothing that forces the second party to agitate for cannabis law reform after it achieves representation.

A Party is a Subset of the Movement

This handbook is for cannabis law reform activism. Much of it is devoted to building a cannabis law reform party for the simple reason that this is an extremely effective way to achieve the objectives of the movement. With enough representation a cannabis law reform party could simply enact legislation that removed cannabis prohibition. With less representation a party could negotiate with a larger party; they could promise to support a larger party on all issues in exchange for the support of that party on cannabis law reform.

The reality is that many people who are interested in cannabis law reform have no interest in party politics. They may believe that a party has no chance of achieving power, or they may have no confidence in the honesty and ability of the people in the party, or they may have extreme distaste for the political system, or they may believe that other methods of enacting cannabis law reform are more effective.

To the extent that non-party activities such as political lobbying are useful, they are strengthened dramatically by any success that a cannabis law reform party achieves. An attempt to lobby a politician is, to some extent, an attempt to persuade them that they could get more votes if they supported a certain policy. If very few people vote for a cannabis law reform party, lobbyists have little ability to persuade politicians.

The cold truth is that without influence over at least some of the legislative body, a cannabis law reform movement is very limited. It can attempt to persuade representatives from other parties that cannabis law reform is a good idea, and without breaking the law there is little else it can do. In practice, a major party that accepts donations from any business threatened by cannabis law reform will never pay more than lip service to the movement. If major parties on both sides of the centre are accepting money from these businesses, the chance of reform is very close to zero.

It may be desirable for a cannabis law reform movement to divide into a party that contests elections and an arm that uses other means. This division naturally suggests itself once the question of civil disobedience is raised.

The Danger of Splitting Support

At an absolute minimum, a cannabis law reform party must aim to get votes from everyone in the cannabis law reform movement. Experience has shown that a large number of people within the movement may choose to not vote for the cannabis law reform party, and usually for two reasons. The first is that they have little confidence in the ability of the party or the people in it, and the second is that they are afraid the party will fail to achieve representation and as a consequence their vote will be wasted.

Regarding the first reason, the cannabis law reform party must realise that it cannot take any votes for granted. Merely claiming to agitate for cannabis law reform does not give the party the right to expect votes from anyone; they must still prove themselves to be effective and competent. If the members of the national executive do not take their roles seriously, people will vote for others who will.

Regarding the second reason, the party must make people understand that even if it does not achieve representation there are still good reasons to vote for it. The first reason is that there may be something of a herd mentality around voting decisions. No-one likes to back a loser, but the converse of this is that people are much more likely to vote for the party if they think it can win. If a party gets two percent of the popular vote, it may fail to achieve representation, but it has a much better chance in the next election than if it had only half a percent. The second reason is that, the better the party does, the more seriously it (and its policies) will be taken by the other parties. This is crucial for influencing those other parties. An excellent election result might persuade one of the major parties to prioritise cannabis law reform, which means the party can achieve its objectives without representation.

The Question of Civil Disobedience

There is a natural and pragmatic division in any cannabis law reform movement: some people will be interested in civil disobedience as a method of protest and others will not. Those who are not might be more attracted to a cannabis law reform party.

From the beginning, both a cannabis law reform party and a movement must decide if it will officially support civil disobedience, if it will unofficially support civil disobedience, or if will not support civil disobedience.

A cannabis law reform party might openly support and engage in civil disobedience. This has the advantage of strengthening solidarity and resolve amongst those in the movement. It does, however, have some disadvantages. One is the potential for scaring away supporters who are afraid of the legal consequences of civil disobedience. Another is the fact that a party that engages in civil disobedience provides the justice system with weapons that can be used against people in the party or potentially the party itself. If a member of the party engages in civil disobedience near to an election, they leave the party open to the consequences of having that member arrested. That member may then be imprisoned at the time they are most needed on the outside to fight the election.

A party might openly declare that it does not support civil disobedience. This will have the advantage of deflecting legal attacks away from the party, although it has the disadvantage of making the party look weak, as if it is afraid to support the others in the movement who do engage in it. The crucial determinant is that no matter how hard the justice system cracks down on civil disobedience, they cannot touch the party if it is not involved.

A pragmatic compromise is to try and get the best of both worlds by not openly supporting and engaging in civil disobedience but still helping to facilitate and organise it. In reality, many members of any cannabis law reform party will be members of other organisations within the movement, and these organisations may well engage in civil disobedience. It is highly likely that any cannabis law reform party will at least be aware of any major acts of civil disobedience, and anyone who partakes in them could have become aware of them through contacts in the party.

The movement, or at least the people in the party, must find a balance between the benefits and the drawbacks of civil disobedience to the cause.

The Objectives and Opportunities of a Cannabis Law Reform Party

With a set of core values and a target demographic established, a cannabis law reform party can begin to determine its objectives. Although the ultimate objective is to enact cannabis law reform, a large number of other objectives must be achieved before this is possible.

At a bare minimum, it intends to get its leader into the legislative body. In a mixed member proportional system such as New Zealand, there may be a threshold of support that must be crossed for the party to get any seats. For example, if the Aotearoa Legalise Cannabis Party does not win an electorate seat, it must gain at least 5% of the votes in a general election, which would result in a minimum of six seats. If this was achieved it could take the Leader, the Deputy Leader, the Treasurer, the President, the Secretary and the Membership Secretary into Parliament.

The party could potentially achieve cannabis law reform without representation in the legislative body. This could happen when politicians of other parties take note of a rapidly expanding cannabis law reform movement. It could happen purely by coincidence. Regardless of these possibilities, the party should set representation as its ultimate objective.

The Opportunities of a Cannabis Law Reform Movement Outside Those Offered to a Party

Although this handbook focuses heavily on the construction and operation of a cannabis law reform party, the movement itself is bigger than this. Some of the activity of members of the movement may be focused around lobbying the other parties, or increasing support for cannabis law reform amongst voters with no reference to the party itself.

Lobbying is an art in itself and this handbook does not have the scope to investigate it. It is enough to say that a large part of lobbying lies in persuading politicians that they could increase their share of the vote if certain policies were adopted. Obviously, therefore, the position of any lobbyist will be far stronger if they can point to electoral success on the part of the cannabis law reform party.

It is always possible for a member of the movement to increase the chances of cannabis law reform by promoting a party, other than the cannabis law reform party, who can nonetheless be expected to take action on behalf of reform. An example of this might be efforts to persuade social democrat voters to vote for an environmentalist party that has cannabis law reform as one of its policies. The chief danger of this is that, in doing so, a voter is supporting a number of policies that may take precedence over cannabis law reform.

It is absolutely crucial that the party has the support of the wider movement. Experience has shown that even environmentalist parties who profess a strong belief in social justice will abandon cannabis law reform if they decide it is too difficult (of course, they will not admit to this). If cannabis law reform is seen as a fringe issue - and it often is, even in cases where a majority of the population is for it - then parties will quickly abandon it if they decide to make a move towards the centre.

Law Reform or Advocacy?

Another decision that will have to made is the extent to which the cannabis law reform movement will seek to advance the cause of cannabis users beyond changing the cannabis laws. The movement can limit itself to law reform, or it can branch into fighting for the rights of cannabis users across society as a whole.

The latter is called cannabis advocacy, and it involves making sure that cannabis users are aware of their rights.

It may also involve giving free legal advice (make sure it is good), or campaigning to break down prejudices that the mainstream may hold against cannabis users.

Giving legal advice is difficult if there is no-one in the movement who is a qualified lawyer specialising in cannabis issues. If the movement knows someone who is, that person could benefit considerably from having clients referred to them, and may be willing to reciprocate in the form of free legal advice in other areas.

It is hard to be effective with anti-prejudice action because of the vast numbers of people holding inaccurate views of cannabis, its use or its users. Nevertheless, there are numerous opportunities for action. If a newspaper article paints some cannabis users as stupid, there is an opportunity for an angry letter pointing out the use of stereotype.

Creating a Party Constitution

When the embryonic movement has agreed to fight for cannabis law reform, and when it has agreed on its core values, the final step before recruiting members is the creation of a party constitution. In some territories this is a legal requirement for the party to be recognised as a party, but even if it is not a constitution is vital for the party.

If a cannabis law reform party has a constitution to which any member can refer, it will have a method of guiding action at all times and at all levels. At a minimum the party constitution ought to declare the purpose and goals of the party and how it intends to achieve them. A well-written constitution will prevent any rogue element within the party from illegally taking power, and will simplify and harmonise the action of all of its members. In cases where there is a dispute over powers, the constitution is the final arbiter.

The constitution ought to declare the structure of the party executive and how these roles are to be filled. It ought to declare what must be done in any situation in which the party finds itself. It ought to declare what the roles of every member of the executive is, how a citizen becomes a legal member of the party, and what the rights and responsibilities of all members are. It ought to declare how party officials are to conduct themselves and how official party meetings are run.

Care must be taken to ensure that the constitution is not unduly restrictive. It must make provision for changing circumstances and political environments so that the party can most effectively grow and adapt. It must also make provision for how it is to be altered should it become necessary, although, for obvious reasons, this must not be made too easy.

2. MEMBERSHIP

The Purpose and Goals of a Membership System

The objective of a party membership system is to increase the effectiveness of the party to the point that it can enact cannabis law reform. To this end the party will require enough members so that it can carry out the necessities of survival, so that it can attract membership fees to help run and promote the party, and so that it can campaign on behalf of the party policy and win enough electoral support to take some power in the political system.

Regarding the necessities of survival, the party must do the things it needs to do to be legally recognised as a political party and to legally contest elections. If electoral law in the territory the party is in requires that the party maintain a certain number of members, this number must be maintained. If electoral law demands that the party must complete certain paperwork, this must be done. Usually there will be paperwork relating to the registration of the party and registration of the party's intent to contest an election.

Membership fees are discussed at length in "Cost of Membership" below. To simplify, membership fees must cover the cost of the Membership Office, with enough left over to allow the Fundraising Officer to assume operation.

The Motives for Joining a Cannabis Law Reform Party

Every individual who joins the cannabis law reform movement does so for their own reasons. Although some of these reasons may be the same as for other members, the degree of importance attached to each reason might not be the same. Although the reasons for an individual to join are not as important as the fact that they do join, these reasons need to be understood by the party executive if the members are to be retained in the party and used most effectively.

Some might join the movement for social reasons. They might get a sense of camaraderie out of fighting the system, and they might be more concerned with gatherings and events than they are with fundraising. People like this are great for increasing the membership base of the movement and for making sure that protests and gatherings are well attended. Some of them might have a huge number of like-minded friends on Facebook and can send them all a message at short notice.

Some might join the movement for ideological reasons. They are usually people who have a considerable understanding of the political system and who have strong opinions about liberty or social justice. People like this are great for developing party policy and for ensuring that the movement works as efficiently as possible. The danger with this sort of person is that the more ideologically inclined they are, the more fanatical they are likely to be. It is great if they are fanatical about cannabis law reform only, but in practice they will have other agendas.

Some might join the movement for financial reasons, although these people are relatively few. Many of these people will be motivated by the potential profits in large-scale hemp farming or in running cannabis cafés. These people are great for putting forward the economic arguments for cannabis law reform, and in special cases they may be able to influence someone with money to make a considerable donation to the movement.

Some might join the movement as an expression of rebellion. These people are often unified in opposition to the police or the courts, or even any kind of authority itself. Their contribution to the movement is often a double-edged sword. While they might be excellent at increasing support and action for the movement, they might not listen to party officials who tell them that some of their behaviour is counterproductive. They might be very charismatic but have extensive criminal records and a criminal mentality.

Some might join the movement simply because they are cannabis users and prefer to associate with other cannabis users. Given that, under a system of prohibition, confessing to cannabis use is also confessing that one is a criminal, a large proportion of people in the cannabis law reform movement will be like this. This category of person will have a large influence on the solidarity of the movement, and if the movement can successfully portray itself as a haven for stoners it will do very well.

As can be seen from this limited overview, people will come to the movement for a vast number of reasons and combinations of reasons. The challenge for the national executive is to bring this diversity together into an effective political force, and the better it understands the needs and wants of its members the more effective it will be. It is vital for the party executive to keep in mind that anyone who comes to the movement can be of use in repealing cannabis prohibition.

The Cost of Membership

Regarding membership fees, this might initially form a large part of the necessary funding to get the party off the ground and carrying out the necessities of survival. The party (or at least its Membership Secretary) must decide what the financial cost of membership should be, whether there should be differing tiers of membership and how much these must cost.

At a minimum the cost of membership should cover the physical costs of receiving and processing membership applications. This would therefore cover postbox rental, compensation (if any) of the persons tasked with processing the applications, and cost of any correspondence (if any). Regarding the cost of correspondence, one might expect at least a letter containing a membership card, a welcome letter, some policy information and instructions on who to contact should further correspondence be desired. This entails printing costs, and the cost of envelopes and stamps. These costs are unlikely to be major.

Regarding the actual cost of standard membership, the party might wish to choose a price that maximised the amount of money that could be collected in membership fees. This raises an immediate point: some people are able or willing to pay more than others.

Having a tiered membership system has several advantages. The most obvious one is the case of having unwaged discounts for membership. The optimal price for standard membership might be based on an amount an employed person could pay. An unwaged discount saves the party from missing out on money and members because the price of standard membership is too high.

The opposite of the discount membership is the "enthusiast" membership. At the very least, such a membership would allow a member to feel that they had made a greater than average contribution to the financial success of the party. The member will feel that their contribution is appreciated if they receive some merchandise, even if this is just a pen or a policy booklet that the standard members don't get.

Over and above the financial benefits of having a tiered system of membership, it allows the party to organise more effectively. Unwaged members may be too poor to have time to offer the party, or they could be on a benefit that gave them money to live and significant spare time to spend on the party. Unwaged members are also the least likely to support the party with donations, so can potentially be excluded from future fundraising correspondence.

Standard members might have money to spend on membership, but less time to devote to party issues (because of work). Also because of employment issues they may be unwilling to attract publicity for the movement in case of reprisal.

Enthusiast members are the best bet for both fundraising and for volunteer work. The party Fundraising Officer might wish to send out regular merchandise offers to these people, perhaps at discount rates in appreciation of the member paying the enthusiast cost. They are also good to target when an election approaches, for at this time they will be most enthusiastic about donating money.

Methods of Recruiting Members

Once a membership system is in place, consideration can be given to the various methods of recruiting members. Traditionally members were recruited when activists persuaded people they met face-to-face to join the movement. Usually this involved getting a filled out membership form that would then be passed on the Membership Secretary along with some cash. The essential requirement here is that the Membership Secretary is able to process these applications.

In a modern context it can also be effective to attract members through the party website, although for legal reasons they may not be allowed to join by simply filling out an electronic form. If much of the merchandise sold contains the party website address this will in turn attract people who might join the party. A major advantage of this method is that it makes handling income of membership fees much easier, for the main reason that money must go through the hands of fewer people.

If the website is used as a main recruitment tool it becomes necessary for the Webmaster and the Membership Secretary to have close co-operation. The party Treasurer might oversee the monies collected, and might be in charge of the system of payment that online applications use.

It is far easier to attract members if the recruiting agent can explain not only the personal benefits of joining the movement but also party policy and the potential personal benefits of enacting legislation that the party is proposing. For these reasons any party member tasked with recruitment should be familiar with Parts Two and Three of this book. Also for these reasons, the party needs an Information Officer who can provide recruitment agents with documents that can be handed out to anyone interested.

The Movement Can Win Through Air or Ground Power

With a membership system in place, anyone whose attention can be brought to the party could join it and starting agitating on its behalf. There are two different strategies for starting a law reform movement, and they approximate the use of air power and ground power in conventional warfare.

Using air power means to hit the media. To some extent this requires money, but social media (as discussed below) offers great returns for the expense. Before spending any large sum of money on a media campaign, it's vital that the party understands which demographic it is targeting.

Another way of looking at air power is that it operates on the national level. The idea is to get the national

Executive into the legislative body, with the hope that they can negotiate their way to cannabis law reform once inside.

Using ground power means to start small and build into a force. It might mean that one person starts talking about cannabis law reform at their pub or workplace. They need not even agitate directly for the party (and in some cases that is preferable), but if they raise the issue of cannabis law reform, and anyone becomes interested, that person will find the party.

Another way of looking at ground power is that it operates on the local level. The wonder of it is that three guys at a pub who agree that something should be done about cannabis prohibition can be the first flicker of ground power. The next step is to agitate for cannabis law reform, then run a candidate for a local body election, then for a state election, and so on up.

The main difference between the two is that, just like in conventional warfare, air power is useless unless it is followed up with ground troops. If the party is flooded with support and volunteers after a mass media campaign, it is crucial that they become involved with the party structure enough so that they can become effective activists themselves.

It is crucial to emphasise that both of these approaches are necessary to success. It doesn't matter how much people talk about cannabis law reform if no-one is taking action, and it doesn't matter how much money is spent in the media if no-one is persuaded to take action.

Getting Maximum Value Out of Each New Member

Each time a new member joins the movement there is an opportunity to improve the party. For each individual this opportunity is the greatest the sooner it is to the act of joining, as this is when enthusiasm will be the highest. Because of this, an efficient party bureaucracy is essential.

There are three major objectives from the point of view of the Membership Office. It must gather as much money and information it can from the new member; it must deliver as much information about the party as it can to the new member; and it must do so as quickly as possible. It is worth looking at each of these points in turn.

An element of the first point (the maximisation of income from the new member) has already been discussed. A second element of the first point is information. The application process is an opportunity to find out what skills the new member might have, what resources they can offer to the party, and how much time they are willing to volunteer. With this information the Membership Secretary can direct the member's enthusiasm to where it is the most effective. Anyone with a wide social circle or advanced social skills might be tasked with recruitment of new members. If they have business skills they might be suited for work in the Merchandise Office. People with computer skills could assist the Webmaster.

The second point is giving the new member as much information as they can make use of. There are two areas of information that a new member might be especially interested in. The first is information about the structure of the party, so that the new member can decide where they would most like to help out. The second area is information about party policy, so that the new member can be as effective as possible in winning support in the form of new members, donations or votes.

Information regarding the first area could be tailored to the information given in the member's application form. At a minimum, the member should receive information about the representatives of the party at all levels relevant to that member. They should know who represents the local branch of the party, who represents the regional branch and who represents the national branch. This entails being given contact information about the executive of the branch and of the national party body.

Information regarding the second area would be aimed at educating the new member to become as effective as possible an agent for cannabis law reform. This would involve at least informing them of party policy. In order to become effective at persuading non-members to support the movement, a member has to understand party policy on the issues relevant to its supporters. For this reason, new members should be sent material in the form of either a comprehensive party policy document or smaller, more concise pamphlets that cover an area of special interest.

The third point is that these two steps must be carried out as quickly as possible. If there is a long turnaround time between applying for membership and receiving acknowledgement, the new member might come to think the party is inefficient or has even misappropriated the membership fee. The initial wave of enthusiasm must be ridden.

Motivating New and Old Members to Agitate for Cannabis Law Reform

Everyone in the cannabis law reform movement is ultimately motivated by the benefits of living in a society without prohibition. But if this alone was enough, the cannabis law reform movement would be much larger than it is. If the party President is tasked with motivating the members of the party to action, they should know the basics of the psychology of motivation.

Imagine that all people ask themselves, before taking any action whatsoever, "What's in it for me?" Motivation is a way of answering that question.

Money is always a major motivator, but a party has to be very cautious in using it. If someone is volunteering to do something, don't pay someone else to do it (unless quality is a concern). This is not only a waste of money but, more importantly, people who volunteered will feel like suckers and the pool of volunteer labour will diminish.

Status might be a bigger motivator in societies who do not want for money. The interesting thing about status is that it is to some degree awarded democratically and a person may have it and not know it (or not have it and not know it). Because one person's value of another's status depends on what the first has heard about the second, every time any cannabis law reform activist talks about another one they are giving their value of that person's status. If an activist's status increases, they need only become aware of which action they took that caused this, and they will be motivated to take more such action in the future.

A third major motivator is power, and this is especially true of the kind of person who will join a political party. A cannabis law reform party will not offer its members the kind of power craved by those who would be king, and this raises a couple of points. The first one is that the extreme unlikelihood of a cannabis law reform party achieving an absolute majority in a legislative body will lower the motivation of many people. The second one may be counterintuitive, but it is a fact that many people will be more vicious the lower the stakes are. The reason for this is, if a person desires a certain level of power, and the organisation they are in is small and weak, they must try and control it utterly in order to be satisfied.

The Structure at a National, Regional and Branch Level

Once the national executive is determined, the party can be built to maximise its reach. The national executive is not necessarily the first level of the structure that will be filled in - it is possible that independent groups committed to cannabis law reform will have formed at a local level and will only find out about each other once a move to establish a national body is made. Whatever comes first, the fact is that a national executive must be established before any meaningful progress can be made.

The nature of the regional level of organisation will depend on the territory in which cannabis is to be legalised. Regardless of the size of the territory, any party officers tasked with organisation on a regional level will initially be concerned with growing the party at a branch level. Their primary concern is that the branches within their region are capable of assisting the objectives of the national executive. The regional level is the least important of the three and, if resources are limited, it can survive and be effective with fewer people than at the other two levels.

The branch level is the lowest level of organisation. Ideally, the branch will represent one electorate. This means that it is the responsibility of the branch to elect a candidate from amongst its members to contest any election.

This three-level structure requires a considerable amount of co-operation in order to function effectively. Even if the national body takes care of itself, the regions and branches may need to come under some degree of supervision. To this end, the regional officers have two core roles. They must ensure that every branch within their region operates as it should, and that the national executive receives as much information as they need about the branches.

Reaching Out Internationally

With a national structure established, the movement will have to decide on the degree to which it seeks out and maintains international links. There are several advantages to doing this.

The first is that it becomes possible to learn about how cannabis law reform movements have succeeded or failed in other places and what can be learned from these efforts. News of any success or failure can be communicated to the party membership in an effort to stimulate action or at least debate.

The second is that it becomes easier both to organise speaking tours and conferences, and to attract a higher profile of speaker to each. Many cannabis law reform activists around the world are happy to come and speak about the movement and its objectives, but money is often a problem. With established links it becomes easier to organise events that pay themselves off.

A final advantage is more pertinent to activists in small countries. The international cannabis law reform movement can benefit greatly from law reform anywhere in the world, because information from this can be used in support of the cannabis law reform argument. This means that large organisations in large countries could, at comparatively small expense, donate a game-changing amount of money to a sister organisation in a smaller country.

Organising Members into a National Party Structure

Initially, at least, the party must have defined roles for a number of positions, and members willing to carry out the roles and responsibilities of these positions. A lack of defined roles will maximise interference from other members and will minimise responsibility.

To have a national executive even charitably worthy of

the name, there must be people willing to act as: Leader, President, Secretary and Treasurer. As members join the movement, new positions can be created to delegate responsibility and power and most effectively use the new members' time and energy. The obvious examples here are Deputy Leader, Membership Secretary, Fundraising Officer, Press Secretary, Webmaster and Information Officer.

The Leader should be the public face of the party. They are usually the top-ranked party member and usually have more influence than any other individual member. At important media events, the party will expect the Leader to represent the party. The Leader might not be expected to engage heavily with individual members for the reason that they could be more effective using their time in attempts to get media coverage. The party Leader needs to have an immaculate grasp of party policy and the consequences of implementing it.

The role of the Deputy Leader might be to complement the Leader or to act as a suitable replacement should that become necessary. At a minimum, the Deputy Leader must be able to adequately perform any and all of the roles demanded of the Leader.

Much of the actual leadership of the party is the responsibility of the President. At a minimum the President must ensure that the party Executive is functioning the way it should be. To achieve this they must be intimately familiar with the rights and responsibilities of each office. They must be able to charm, cajole and coerce office holders to do their jobs. If any member of the party has a dispute with another member that cannot be resolved, they ought to be able to turn to the President for mediation.

The role of the Secretary is to ensure that the party complies with the party's legal responsibilities so that the party can continue to exist and to fight elections. Because of this, the Party Secretary is often the one responsible for the most crucial work. Without an effective Secretary, the efficiency of the party will be crippled. The Secretary is responsible for filing the necessary paperwork so that the party legally registers as a political party and so that it can legally contest an election. The Secretary may also be responsible for applying for government funding for media expenses, in so far that it is applicable. If the party must make a yearly declaration that it has the members necessary to qualify as a political party, the Secretary will be responsible for this. In most cases, should the government wish to contact the party they will do so through the Secretary. For this reason, the Secretary must be a person who is contactable at any time and who can be relied upon to transmit any important information to the relevant office holder or the party membership.

The role of the Treasurer is to keep accurate records of and to safekeep the party's finances. At a minimum the Treasurer needs to be aware of the financial resources that the party can bring to bear, and to ensure that these resources are not wasted or misappropriated. The Treasurer must ensure both that the Membership Office is returning money to the party and that it has sufficient resources with which to operate. Both of these considerations also apply to the Treasurer's involvement with the Merchandise Office and the Media Team. The

Treasurer is expected to be able to make competent decisions on what the party can and cannot afford, and how its resources are best utilised.

The role of the Membership Secretary is to keep accurate records of and to safekeep the party's membership records. At a minimum the Membership Secretary must have records of who is and who is not a legal member of the party. The Membership Secretary plays a crucial role in getting the maximum effectiveness out of each new member. They will usually be either the first or the second official contact person that a new member encounters within the party structure, for the reason that they are responsible for any new member receiving party correspondence. The Membership Secretary need not have close contact with new members after they have joined, but they are responsible for making sure that someone does. A more detailed discussion of this role is discussed below in the section "Special Considerations for the Membership Secretary."

The role of the Fundraising Officer is to ensure that the party has access to as much money as it needs to fight elections effectively. In practice there is no upper limit to how much money a movement could use, and indeed a vast majority of elections are won by the parties that spend the most money. The party fundraising system is discussed in detail in section three of this part of the book ("Fundraising"), but to put it simply, the Fundraising Officer is concerned mostly with merchandise and with donations.

The role of the Press Secretary is to ensure that the party maximises its opportunities for media exposure. The art of doing so is discussed in detail in section four of this part of the book ("Media"), but the core of their role is to ensure that the media does its part in promoting the party message. At a minimum, the Press Secretary is responsible for passing official party press releases to the appropriate outlets and co-coordinating interviews between the media and party officials.

The role of the Webmaster is to ensure that the party has an Internet presence that can promote the party policy, provide contact details to party officials in case potential members or media representatives wish for more information, and, crucially, to organise a large part of the party's communication (which is discussed in the section "Special Considerations for the Webmaster").

The role of the Information Officer (informally Propaganda Minister) is to collect party resources in the form of information, in much the same way that the Treasurer collects party resources in the form of money. A more detailed discussion of this role is discussed below in the section "Special Considerations for the Information Officer."

Special Considerations for the Membership Secretary

The truth of running a cannabis law reform party is that its most valuable resource, even greater than the constitution and the website, is its membership records. There are two reasons for this.

The first reason is that the membership records are, in effect, a record of who the party is. If an individual has not applied to the Membership Secretary for membership, or if they have not met the criteria for membership (such as payment), or if their membership has expired, they are not a member of the party. Related to this is the fact that almost all of the organisation of the party must, even if only briefly, go through the Membership Secretary. For anyone to hold any role within the party structure, they must at least be able to show that they are a member, and only the Membership Secretary and the Secretary will be able to confirm this.

The second reason is that the membership records are, in practice if not in theory, mostly a list of criminals, as well as contact details and physical addresses of those criminals. For this reason they are of considerable financial value to certain interests. Agents of the police force might be interested in such a record, as might people who wish to use it to sell cannabis. The Membership Secretary must absolutely ensure that the records do not fall into the wrong hands.

The Membership Secretary must not keep loose copies of the membership records lying around on data sticks or on shared computers, and must not email the records to anyone. The best practice is for the Membership Secretary to keep the records private and secret from all other entities, even those within the party, with the sole exception of the party Secretary, whose confidence the Membership Secretary needs in order to perform their role.

Having said this, elements of the membership records can be shared in limited circumstances, if the principle of compartmentalisation is adhered to. The Webmaster needs to know the names and email addresses of individual members so that they can email them their username and login details for the party website. If any regional or branch officers are tasked with personally welcoming new members to the party, they need to be given names and telephone numbers or email addresses. The Fundraising and Information Officers need the names and addresses of party members in order to send them merchandise or printed information.

Because of the criminal nature of cannabis, potential members must have confidence that their records will be kept private and secret. For this reason it is important that the membership forms declare, in a place where it will be read, that the member's full details are to be seen only by the Membership Secretary and the party Secretary.

If the Membership Secretary, for any reason, fields a request from a person who wants information about specific members of the party, and if requests for this information have not been previously granted by that member, the Membership Secretary should refer this to the party Secretary. The Membership Secretary must always be vigilant to any social engineering that may occur with a view to gaining unauthorised access to the records. Anyone claiming to represent the Police, the Electoral Commission, the Ministry of Justice etc. should be given no more than the contact details for the party Secretary.

Extraordinary Considerations for the Membership Secretary

The Membership Secretary should also maintain a

number of lists. One group of these is of members and certain information about them, and the other is of non-members and their relationships to the party. It ought to be possible, if a spreadsheet is used to keep track of these groups, to sort the people in them according to their location. With several lists of people grouped by their use to the party and by location, the party Executive has a powerful tool with which to coordinate action.

Of the first group there are several different lists depending on what information is needed.

The first of them is a list of members who have signed up a large number of other members. Because a core focus of the Membership Secretary's action is expanding the party, it is important to identify the human avenues through which this ought to be done. If it should be desirable to recruit new members in a certain area, the person most likely to achieve this can be identified and incentivised.

The second is a list of people who have donated their labour. Because a cannabis law reform movement will always have a need for labour it is good to know who can be counted on. This is especially important as an election day draws near and it becomes necessary to have volunteer teams who deposit pamphlets in all of the letterboxes in a certain area. Counsel from the elders of the party also counts as labour, and it is important that the national Executive know who they can count on when advice is needed.

The third is a list of people who have helped with

donations. This is really two sublists, one of those who have donated money and one of those who have solicited it. Although it is important that financial donors are not harassed to donate more, it is good to have a list because most people will want to donate again when an election approaches.

The fourth is a list of people who can provide accommodation for travelling party officials. Because these places will often be safe houses for cannabis consumption, organising a network of such places is like building an Underground Railroad. The first stage of such a network will arise naturally from the interactions between members of the Executive, but, as the party grows, more places will become available.

The fifth is a list of people and their areas of special policy interest. These could be any of the twenty-six points from the section "A Twenty-Six Point Plan" or they could be any others. If new member declares on their membership application that they have a special policy interest, these people can then be contacted should the party wish to make a submission on a certain area.

Finally there are lists of members for any other reason that it might be advantageous to keep a list. There could be any number of such lists, and reasons for them will increase as the party grows and as an election approaches.

Any member not on one of the above lists is a passive member. They are there to pay subs and for the chance that they might become active at some point in the future.

Of the second group there are also several lists.

The first of these is a list of supporters. These are people who will probably vote for the cannabis law reform party but are not members and do not wish to be active in party affairs. They might buy a lot of merchandise, especially at the group level. They might also be happy to receive pamphlets and other party propaganda, and may even be able to pass these on to other supporters. They may even be some of the party's biggest donors.

The second of these is a list of known politicians and their attitudes towards cannabis law reform. The reason for this is covered in the section "Letters to Representatives."

The third of these is a list of private enterprises who have skills that the party could need in the future, and who will either volunteer these skills or trade them for cash. Although much of the labour needs of the party can be met through unskilled and volunteer labour, there will be occasions on which an expert hand is required. Screenprinting, advertising, merchandising and erecting billboards or posters are all examples of skills that the party may need come election time.

Special Considerations for the Webmaster

There are essentially three ways that party members can share information. They can speak to each other, they can write each other letters or they can communicate using the party website. While political parties have functioned for centuries using only the first two methods, using a website as a central basis for communication offers certain advantages that can vastly increase the party's effectiveness.

If the Webmaster builds a site using a modern content management system such as Drupal or Joomla it is possible for every member of the party to have a unique user account that can access areas of the site closed to the public. It is also possible for certain members (such as those on the executive) to have access to areas closed to regular members.

A core responsibility of the Webmaster is to build a forum into the website to facilitate communication. In this way, the party can use a large number of virtual messageboards on which members can post information. The website should also have a private messaging system that can be used for any member who does not wish to make their message public or semi-public.

There are essentially three levels of security that need to be built into the website in order for it to achieve its maximum effectiveness.

The first is the public level, accessible to anyone. The front page of the website, which shares party and cannabis-related news, should be readable by all. It is vital that the front page is updated often enough that people make a regular habit of coming back to it for updates. In this way a following can quickly be created. As long as it is not overrun by trolls or spam, there should be a public forum in which supporters who are not members, or neutrals who wish to find out more about the party, can put questions to party officials and have them answered.

The second is the member level, accessible only to party members. They can read anything that is available to the wider public, and have special access to certain subforums. If the party is to compete on a national level it is vital that the Webmaster set up a subforum for each branch of the party. Any party member should have the ability to post information in a branch's subforum so that members within that branch can organise themselves and share information. Branch officials can give notice of branch meetings through these subforums or they can use them to find out when and where a meeting should take place.

The third is the executive level, accessible only to party officials. They can read anything that is available to the wider public or to members, and have special access to an executive forum. With an executive forum it becomes much easier to plan, inform and discuss strategy. The Membership Secretary can make posts informing the executive of the party's reach and depth in any geographical area, the Treasurer can keep the executive aware of the party's finances, and the Fundraising Officer can let people know when there is new merchandise available for sale.

It is also important that each executive position has responsibility for a subforum named after their role, so that members of the party or of the public can put questions to them and get them answered.

When the party becomes big enough it will need to have

chatrooms in which extensive discussions can take place in a short time period. Every level of security can have its own chatroom if desired.

Special Considerations for the Information Officer

The overall objective of the Information Officer is to make party policy available to members and to the public, so that they will be encouraged to intensify their support for cannabis law reform. To this end, information must be gathered, analysed and disseminated.

Regarding the gathering of information, the first task of the Information Officer is to build a library. Any Internet information pertaining to cannabis or to cannabis law reform ought to be collected into a folder. Copies of any court report from a cannabis case ought to be collected. Information about the different voting districts and their returns for the cannabis law reform party ought to be collated.

Regarding the analysis of information, any willing member of the party could spent hours crunching information, but the Information Officer ought to keep a record of all of the results. Most important is a record of voting demographics. If voting data is compared to Census data it is possible to determine which demographics within a certain area are most likely to favour cannabis law reform (and which areas are most likely to favour cannabis law reform based on their demographics).

Regarding the dissemination of information, the

Information Officer must produce easily copyable documents that explain party policy in core areas. These can then be emailed to supporters or posted out so that they can be photocopied. To take a longer view, the Information Officer can produce merchandise, such as a policy booklet.

If information documents are produced in pamphlet form, there can be dozens of different ones. In principle, any area that cannabis law reform impacts on and about which three hundred words could be written could be a pamphlet, and less if space is taken up with a merchandise or membership panel. Any of the points from "A Twenty-Six Point Plan" in Part Three of this handbook, as well as many others, could be expanded to three hundred words.

Ultimately the Information Officer should seek to produce a policy booklet that can be sold without losing money. The best way to do this is to get every candidate to write a piece about their vision for the cannabis laws. If there are fifty candidates and each writes a three or four page article, the result will be a book that will allow anyone who reads it to be sure of what the party stands for.

Organising Members into Branches

When any new member joins the party, they should be assigned to a branch as part of their entry into the membership records. If there is one branch for every electorate, the membership application should ask the member to declare their electorate and therefore their branch. This process has the potential to become messy if information is not regularly shared between members and if the membership records are not updated. For example, a member might not live in the electorate in which they are enrolled to vote, or they might change their physical address or their electorate.

How the new member is handled will depend on whether their local branch is active.

At the beginning there will be no local branches, although new members can be assigned a branch in expectation that one will soon be created. Two conditions must be met for the creation of a new branch to be approved by the national body. Firstly, it must have enough members so that a meaningful group can be created: this means that there are at least enough people willing to fill the roles of Branch President, Branch Secretary and Branch Treasurer. Secondly, at least one of these members must have the confidence of the national body to perform the required tasks of a branch founder.

Regarding the first condition, a branch must have at an absolute minimum three people, although the national body might like to set a minimum number of members to ensure that the branch can continue activity if one of those members should lose willingness or ability to perform their designated role. Ideally a branch would begin its active life with an election for the three roles, which implies that there are enough members to have competition for these roles and to vote for them.

Regarding the second condition, the national body might like to ensure that the member who takes the initiative in founding a branch is both capable of doing so and is of sufficient character that they will do so in a way that assists the party to achieve its objectives. For this reason it is useful to have a process of vetting the new members so that the national executive can decide if these conditions are met. Often a simple phonecall from either the Secretary or the President will be sufficient. Because the member tasked with branch formation will often have considerable influence within that branch, the national executive has an incentive to make sure that member is the right person.

If the new member's local branch is already active, things are much simpler. The Membership Secretary must, as part of the welcome letter sent to the new member, give that member contact details so that they can contact their local branch for more information. Usually these will be the contact details of the Branch Secretary. If the local branch has an officer tasked with welcoming and orientating new members, the Membership Secretary must inform that officer that their branch has a new member. If both the branch officer and the new member are given each other's contact details it is much more likely that the new member will be integrated into the party system in the most effective manner.

Organising Members into Chapters

The next level down from the branch is the chapter. If an electorate is so large that there are significant population centres in more than one place, and that travel between these centres is not desirable, then the party may have to organise its members into chapters. In practice, there is little difference between a branch and a chapter, but, because the branch operates on the level of the electorate, individual chapters will not elect candidates. The chapters must come together at the branch level to elect a candidate (this need not happen if there are local body elections that are best handled by one chapter).

In Some Regards, Action at a Branch Level is Better

No matter how effective the national executive is at framing the argument, at attracting money and at spreading propaganda, there are areas of cannabis law reform that the branch is better suited to. Whatever the qualities of the members of the national executive, there will never be more than a dozen or so of them and their ability to perform face-to-face functions will therefore be very limited.

With the obvious exception of that which occurs at national AGMs, most of the social functions of the party will occur at the branch level. It should not be forgotten that, although the purpose of the movement is to enact cannabis law reform, much of the motivation for individual members to join will be social. Related to this is the fact that much of the effectiveness of the movement will depend on the solidarity between its members. An active and healthy branch will be the best place for social gatherings, because it will put the least travel demands on people.

Because some information is best transmitted face-to-face, the branch offers the ideal location for this, both for individual members and for the party as a whole.

Regarding individual members, the Branch Secretary or

President might take responsibility for educating them about their rights before the law, whether this be at the point of arrest, interrogation or trial. They might be the people to go to if a deeper or broader education in the effects of cannabis prohibition or legalisation is desired. They might be the ones who can offer the best advice if the member wishes to advance cannabis law reform on their own initiative. Crucially, they ought to take on a major responsibility in ensuring that the member feels welcome and appreciated, and that their efforts are useful to the movement and that the movement can and will win.

Regarding the party as a whole, branch officials play an important role in getting to know members on a personal basis. This gives them the ability to vet these members and to pass their impressions of them up to the national executive. In this sense they can achieve two major objectives that are both crucial for the effectiveness of the party as a whole. Firstly, they can suggest to the national executive that certain members are competent and that the party would benefit from giving these members more responsibility. Secondly, they can suggest to the national executive that certain members are incompetent, dangerous or insane, and that the party ought to minimise interactions with these members.

The branch level is also better than the national level at selling merchandise. If there are seventy branches, each with a fundraising officer, then their combined efforts will be far greater than an impersonal website and some brochures.

In Some Regards, Action at a Regional Level is Better

Regional officers are more than a middle layer of bureaucracy. Their role in party function is vital, and it is twofold.

The first is making sure that all of the branches within the region are operating effectively. At a minimum, the regional officer should keep the contact details of all of the branch officers operating within their region. With this done, the regional officers can stay in touch with the branch officers, find out anything they need to know, and inform them of new opportunities to promote either propaganda or merchandise.

The second is making sure that the national Executive can use the branches as effectively as possible. If a new role is created within the party structure, it ought to be filled by someone from the membership, and the regional officers are best placed to recommend to the Executive who these people ought to be.

The Rights and Responsibilities of Office Holders

Office holders have both rights over decision making and responsibilities to the party, to other members and to the law. Without a clear, defined and detailed description of the rights and responsibilities of each role the movement will fall into bickering and arse-covering.

An office holder will have veto rights over action taken in the name of their office. In many cases, the office holder should be open to influence and suggestions from other members but the final say is in their hands. A Membership Secretary must be able to decide the composition of the welcome letters and should have the right to levy the correct membership fees. A Fundraising Officer should have the right to decide which prices will result in the optimal income.

Likewise, office holders will have certain responsibilities, in particular the responsibility to ensure that their role is carried out to the best of their ability. The party must have mechanisms in place so that pressure can be brought to bear on anyone who is not fulfilling their role, and to remove and replace them should that pressure be ineffective. Most of the responsibility for this falls on the Party President. Without clearly defined roles, therefore, the President's job is impossible.

Party Officials may be Elected or Appointed

In some cases, party officials will be elected and in other cases they will be appointed. Because it is best to have a transparent and meritocratic party, it is best if positions are elected whenever possible. Having said this, some positions cannot perform their role if they do not have the confidence of other office holders. The Membership Secretary must have the confidence of the party Secretary, the Fundraising Officer must have the confidence of the Treasurer, and the Webmaster must have the confidence of the Press Secretary. Should the Membership Secretary lose the confidence of the party Secretary, the Secretary must be able to put a process in motion by which the Membership Secretary is replaced.

Whether officials are elected or appointed, there must be a clear way of removing and replacing them in cases of dereliction of duty. Perhaps the best way is for the Executive to vote on whether they have confidence in the ability of that person, and declare them stripped of their office if not.

Unofficial Roles

In practice, a majority of members will not be party officials. Despite this, party officials can increase the effectiveness of their operations if they are able to co-ordinate help from regular members. The job of the Membership Secretary is much easier if they task others with recruiting new members in their area. Likewise, the Fundraising Officer can bring in much more money if they have other people selling merchandise to their friends.

The party itself must decide how many different roles its members can perform and which of them have the right to speak on behalf of the party and in what areas.

In practice, if the party is big enough, it could have a shadow government. Each of the policy areas could have its own spokesperson, who might be known as, for example, the Party Spokesman/woman for Housing. Each of these spokespeople would be responsible for understanding and promoting party policy in their area of expertise.

The advantage of the shadow government system is that a relatively large number of members can work for the party in a semi-official capacity and in defined roles.

This makes it easier for them to target promotion of party policy to those who have the most interest in it. For example, the Party Spokesperson for Youth Affairs could liaise with a magazine targeted at young voters. This will also give the spokesperson a better opportunity to understand the concerns of supporters or voters who are most affected by that area of party policy, and is therefore in a good position to relay that information to whoever is tasked with co-coordinating official policy.

Something that must be approached with caution at all stages is the idea of prestige roles. Even if two members have no official roles, they may have different levels of status and influence within the movement. People who have been in the movement for a long time might demand special respect or deference, particularly if they believe they have influence over someone in a high role, or if they occupied a high role in the past.

An obvious example of a prestige role is Life Membership. Any party member that has contributed considerable time and/or expense towards party success might be declared a Life Member. It is not a good idea to give Life Membership to active members. In cases where it is desired, it is best to award it to a person who has retired from (or been ousted from) an important position. The party may wish to have a "Council of Elders" that consists of Life Members. This is a good way to retain expertise within the system.

What social status is afforded a particular member is a double-edged sword that must be handled with good judgement. Crucially, every member must feel that they and their efforts are respected, and they must understand that decision-making power lies in the hands of those who are tasked with it. If a new member is treated in a patronising or dismissive manner they could leave. If an old member feels that their prior effort is not respected they could also leave.

What needs to be countered, at all stages, is the tendency for people to demand more respect then they deserve. This will have a strongly corrosive effect on party discipline and morale. Anyone claiming to be a "granddaddy" or "guru" of the movement must be treated with suspicion. It needs to be emphasised at all levels of party structure and at all times that respect is granted according to how effectively that person advances the party objectives.

A Party Must Be Meritocratic

A fact of human nature is that most people will desire more influence than their level of competence suggests they ought to have. It is crucial for the success of the party that individuals who can most advance the party's objectives are given the most influence. For one thing, this prevents incompetent people rising to the top and damaging the party's image or its effectiveness in achieving its goals. For another, it prevents competent people from being placed in roles where they can do little to help the party.

Initially, a party might not have competition for certain roles. The membership of the party will expand faster than the number of official roles within it, so as it does it is logical that competition for some roles will increase. When this occurs, situations will arise in which a member believes themselves more capable of performing a certain role than the incumbent, or they might believe that another member is more competent at a certain role than the incumbent.

A party must have a mechanism through which members can challenge for positions and to be granted them if they have enough support from other members. No member can become conflated with the role they play in the party. No matter how long a member has been in a role, that role is not that member: that member is, and only temporarily, that role.

There are two major advantages to a meritocratic system. The most obvious is that it ensures the effectiveness of members is matched to their influence. The second, more subtle reason has to do with party morale. If a member feels that their efforts will be recognised and rewarded they have a much greater incentive to help the movement.

The long term viability of any movement centres around its ability to get the right people into the right positions. Many a political movement was formed by people who were soon thrown out of the way as the movement gathered momentum.

Potential Inefficiencies That Must be Considered

As the movement increases in size, it will begin to attract elements that do not help it achieve its objectives, and may very well attract elements that make it less effective. There are two major ways that an individual within the party might be less than optimally effective.

The first is if the individual is not competent enough to carry out a useful role within the party, and the second is if the individual has a disintegrative effect on party structure or on party solidarity.

The most obvious of these, incompetent people occupying positions of authority, has been discussed above. The smaller the movement is the more likely this is to be a problem. If the movement is very small, people with a few committed allies can vote themselves into positions of power even if they are unqualified to be there. Also, the smaller the movement is, the more influence can be bought or expected in exchange for donations.

The second phenomenon, which becomes more noticeable later, is the disorganising effect of individual ego on the movement. This phenomenon is not wholly distinct to the first. A person intent on maintaining their position and status at all costs may go as far as to discourage new members joining the party. A person with an excessive ego can alienate other members and lower their enthusiasm for cannabis law reform. The nature of politics attracts egotistical people, and some of them might join the movement asking what the party can do for them, not what they can do for the party.

Both of these problems can be worked around by increasing the size of the movement and by increasing the amount of information that is shared between party members.

Increasing the size of the movement puts pressure on the incumbents. It increases the chance of finding someone who could do a better job than the incumbent, and it increases the outrage if a party role is not carried out in an effective manner.

Increasing the amount of information shared between party members makes it more likely that members will become aware of party inefficiencies and it will guide them as to how to circumvent these problems. For this reason is it vital to have regular meetings, whether these be national conferences, Skype calls or local branch gatherings.

Party Influence Flows Towards the Top

The Party Executive represents, at a minimum, the collective will of the members of the party. Each individual member has the right to expect that party officials will listen to and respect their ideas and suggestions, even if these are not implemented. If a member does not feel that they are respected by the party hierarchy they will lose interest and motivation, and could even become an enemy of the movement.

For this reason, it should be kept in mind at all times that the influence of the party leadership is a direct function of the size and organisation of its membership. The larger the movement is, the more votes, money and energy it will have. The better organised it is, the more effectively it can use those resources. These two factors are so crucial that any member of the movement, whatever their role in it, can work to help it achieve its objectives.

The understanding that party influence flows from the

voters up towards the executive is important. It ensures that the correct attitude towards voters is taken. It also helps people resist the temptation to believe that the strength of the party is in the strength of its leader. The party is not a structure formed by activists that must then persuade, bribe, threaten and coerce voters; rather, the party has formed out of the will of the voters and represents them. If the party does not win representation in the legislative body it is not because stoners didn't turn out to vote but because the party failed to inspire them to do so. This distinction is subtle, but there are rewards for grasping it.

The Nature of Individuals Involved in Cannabis Law Reform

Anyone running a cannabis law reform movement will soon become aware that people who use cannabis and people who are interested in politics are subsets of the general population, and that members of the movement, at least in some ways, are not like people as a whole. This is not to say that all cannabis law reform activists are a certain way; there is far too much diversity in the movement for this claim to be made. Nevertheless, anyone who meets any number of cannabis law reform activists will come to observe certain patterns.

A common lament in the movement is that organising people is "like herding cats." Central to the nature of any cannabis law reform movement is resistance against unwanted authority. If a person in the movement wishes to give direction to anyone else, they must consider this. No one who is angry about police oppression is going to submit to directions from someone with even less authority. Any cannabis law reform movement that is structured on people at the top giving orders to people at the bottom will fail. The people at the top need to put the case for action to everyone else (including each other) and let this lead where it must.

Because cannabis prohibition is enforced by the establishment, many people who come to the cannabis law reform movement will be anti-establishment. Obviously, in order to affect the law, a person must at the very least disagree with the establishment position in that area. If a cannabis law reform movement is to be successful it might have to moderate the anti-establishment extremists within its ranks. Anyone calling for politicians to be killed, or for the state to be entirely dismantled, or claiming that the police force consists entirely of thugs, thieves and rapists, might not be suitable for a spokesperson's position. Whatever the arguments in favour of such positions, they will be considered by the vast majority of people to be extremist positions and promoting them will not help the movement achieve its objectives.

Another consideration is that members of a cannabis law reform movement might have higher than average levels of paranoia. This could be because of the nature of the psychoactive effects of cannabis, or it could be a completely rational response to prohibition, or it could be both. The practical consequences of this phenomenon are that it may be more difficult to convince any potential supporter to put themselves out there. Members might be unwilling to become candidates for fear of provoking police action. Supporters might be unwilling to become members for fear of government forces compromising the membership database and getting their records. Some cannabis users may be unwilling to come out of the cannabis closet for fear of social or work-related reprisals. Activists need to bear in mind that there will be higher than usual levels of paranoia and distrust within the movement and will need to take extra steps to built trust among its members.

Because cannabis possession and supply is (presumably) a crime in the territory in which a cannabis law reform movement operates, a vast majority of its members will be criminals. Although most of these people are only criminals because of cannabis prohibition, an activist in the cannabis law reform movement might well encounter people whose attitudes to welfare fraud, tax evasion, casual violence, and a host of other crimes are relaxed to say the least. This may or may not affect those people's effectiveness as a cannabis law reform campaigner, but the risk is there that the legal system could deal to them, and this may have consequences for the movement.

When these factors are combined, other risks present themselves. If the movement has a heavy criminal element it is entirely possible that activists who are not themselves criminals will not be trusted. They may be suspected of being police informers, undercover police agents or even representatives of the intelligence and security services. Although it is possible that the establishment would have an incentive to infiltrate the movement, excessive paranoia about this possibility could cripple the movement's effectiveness. As with many other considerations, a balance must be found.

Who to Keep an Eye On

Ideas are great, and they are necessary in order to have something to act towards. But the action is more important than the idea. Beware of the activist who comes up with fantastic ideas for other people to work on. They are often the same kind of activist who believes that anything they come up with is gold and the others should be grateful that someone with their vision is present. Sometimes a new member will come to you requesting fifty membership forms for the people he's persuaded to join, and sometimes they will come with what they believe is a game-changing idea that will win the battle straight away. Be cautious of the second type. If the idea also requires most of the movement's funding in order to work, be doubly cautious.

Egomaniacs are similar. Beware of anyone who appears to behave as if they have been sent by God to rid the world of cannabis prohibition. The difference between a movement and a cult is that a movement can continue even if its leaders retire. A cult has followers, a movement has a collective energy that pushes all of its members forwards. Likewise, beware the follower. If a person cannot evaluate the merit of an idea by themselves, they are of little use to the inner circles of the party where many decisions are made.

There are several degrees of egomaniac lower than the full psychopath, and all of them are potentially dangerous to the party. While it is necessary for an activist to have an ego healthy enough to withstand the opprobrium and stupidity of the prohibitionists, beware the activist who ignores the needs of the party to push their own agenda. People who encourage others to take risks that they do not themselves take, people who disrespect the feelings and opinions of others and people who do not seem to understand that it is not morally justified to shoot a police officer for searching your car must all be treated with suspicion.

Be wary of anyone who tries to buy status with money, especially when the party is in its infancy. Depending on the size of its area, the movement may need to spend millions to win, and one person spending a few hundred on their own candidacy is not the next Caesar. It is fair that some status be given to people who aided the party on the financial front, but it has to be kept in proportion. The party never needs a pissing contest around who spent the most money, especially when most of the useful party work is unpaid.

Also be wary of anyone who appears to seek power for its own sake. They will make decisions based on what benefits them and not the movement.

Who to Keep an Eye On II (Divided Loyalties)

Watch out for members of other parties. The fact is that votes are a scarce resource, and any one party could potentially steal votes from another. A consequence of this is that many parties will seek to insert moles within the cannabis law reform movement.

These moles may do nothing other than report back to a superior. They will pass on information relating to the size of the party membership, the financial resources it has, and specific information about people in the party leadership. They may do much more than this, including sabotaging the party's efforts or misleading its members.

The nature of politics is that many people who join a cannabis law reform party will have formerly been members of other parties. These members are valuable because they will pass on information about how the other parties function (or fail to function).

Because many members of the cannabis law reform party will have recently jumped ship, it is not easy to determine straight away who is a mole and who is not. At a minimum, if it comes to the attention of the Membership Secretary that a party member is active in a rival party, or holds a position of responsibility in a rival party, that membership should be revoked and the member expelled.

Another thing to watch out for is people loyal to prohibitionist values. If a person joins the cannabis law reform movement, but is indifferent to rights violations suffered in other areas, their motives will be seen by many as suspicious.

Members Can, and Should, be Recruited With a View to What They Bring to the Movement

This section will make more sense if the activist has read "Extraordinary Considerations of the Membership Secretary" above.

Most people have special skills and advantages, and if the Membership Secretary is grouping people into lists based on these skills they might as well recruit for them.

The most valuable member of all is the one that can bring in the most other members. This is because of the power of exponential growth. To give an example, Jeff Lye of the Waitakere branch of the Aotearoa Legalise Cannabis Party signed up over 200 members in one year in a self-funded campaign. If a hundred people like this could be found, the party would soon grow to a number equivalent to an Army division.

Build it Wide, Build it Deep

One excellent advantage when it comes to building a structure on the national level is that the Membership Secretary can discover the geographical areas where the party is weak and those where it is strong. The party can then funnel some resources from a strong area into a weak one, where they will likely yield better returns.

Even with a skeletal national system, it is possible to specifically target certain areas for recruitment. Any responsible member who intends to pass through the area in question could hit the streets with a clipboard and a couple of hundred membership forms. Because these new members are followed up with merchandise offers, the movement has the potential to go deep quickly.

If there is an election in which a cannabis candidate is standing, that area should be targeted for members and merchandise well in advance. If necessary, activists from neighbouring areas might be able to help.

With a good website, the party can put up a "Members wanted in: " notice, perhaps with some bonus merchandise if they sign up while they live in that area.

Building a Cannabis Law Reform Movement is Essentially a Question of Solidarity

Humans are selfish; this is a point understood by most people when they are children and the balance of information coming from the world does not argue otherwise. When a person becomes older and more sophisticated they realise that, although people are selfish, in many cases they do not behave in purely selfish ways.

The reason for this is that if any one person wants to fuck over a second, the most important thing he can do is to curry favour with a third. If the second can bring a fourth and a fifth into the equation it changes again. And so on, up the chain of order, until one group becomes powerful enough to enforce its will on a certain area of territory with little expectation that this will be challenged. The smaller the opposition, the less likely the status quo will be upset.

This means that the path to victory is for members to fight alongside each other. The more intensely a member feels that the goals of the other members are his own goals, the most enthusiastically he will fight on behalf of the others.

Solidarity Through Brotherhood

A certain distance must be maintained between the membership and anyone not a member. This is not a suggestion to start a cult. It means that there must be something that stays exclusive to members. Of course, only members will have official membership cards, and only official members should attend party meetings. But if it is desirable to add another layer on top of this the Merchandise Officer might have to run some limited edition stock.

An ideal piece of merchandise that will remain exclusive is a cigarette lighter printed with a specific image, such as "Cannabis Party AGM 2012." The Merchandise Officer might have a hundred of these made and hand them out to attendees at the Annual General Meeting.

Another idea is to do a once-yearly t-shirt print run where every participating member gets a t-shirt with their membership number on it, or title such as "Cannabis Party Treasurer 2012." This is also a cheap and easy way of honouring the elders of the party, because their membership numbers will be lower and this will afford them some respect.

Inner Circles, Degrees and Ranking

Everyone who has ever been part of a group will have observed that, no matter the size of the group, there is an inner circle in which important decisions are made, even if this inner circle only consists of one person. The reasons for this are obvious to anyone who has ever considered why there are no national elections or referenda on the question of library fees and parking fines. The human tendency to form social hierarchies expresses itself in the form of political parties as well, and the two most noticeable ones are who knows the most about party operation and who makes the important decisions (and there is high overlap between the two). The natural pattern is that people are higher the more trusted and effective they are.

This handbook cannot cover all of the intrigues of intra-party shitfighting, but this section will outline three ways of minimising the impact of damaging elements within the party membership, once they are identified.

The first is for the party to have inner circles. It appears to be natural for any group to do this. Within the wider group of the membership is a circle of active members, which contains highly effective members, which contains the Executive, which contains the Leader. A member's opinion on party matters will be considered more generously the further the member is up this chain.

The second way is to have a system of degrees. One easy way is to use the forums. Anyone who makes a certain number of posts is asked about how they think they can contribute to the party, and if this appeals to the people already in the degree that new person is admitted.

The third, and most transparent way, is to have a ranking system. The major problem with a ranking system is that it is hard to set up, for the reason that so much as raising the idea divides the party. Having said that, most understand that some roles are more important than others. An example of a ranking system might look like this:

1. Leader
2. Deputy Leader
3. Secretary
4. Treasurer
5. President

6. Membership Secretary
7. Press Secretary
8. Fundraising Officer
9+. Regional Officers

It is best not to get carried away by talk like this. The cannabis law reform movement is a cultural phenomenon, not a criminal conspiracy, and the path to victory lies in understanding that forces have conspired against us, not the other way around. However, there may be times when the information in this passage is necessary for the movement, in particular if there is an organised attempt to infiltrate it.

3. FUNDRAISING

No cannabis law reform movement can be close to maximally effective without money. Although solidarity is free and fundamental, it can only go so far. With money, a cannabis law reform movement can reach far more people with its propaganda. It can cover expenses for party representatives who partake in media opportunities. It can pay people to do work that they would not have done for free.

The triple pillars of any fundraising effort are merchandise, donations and advertising. The major difference is that with merchandise, something physical is exchanged for the financial contribution.

Merchandise

With outsourcing and print-on-demand services it is easy to start a basic Merchandise Office. A decent Merchandise Office will achieve at least two goals: fundraising and expanding membership. There are ways that both goals can be achieved with one action. Party officials in contact with members can persuade them to sell merchandise to like-minded friends and associates. Members can be encouraged with offers of a free t-shirt if they sell nine, for example. In this manner the member becomes used to taking action on behalf of the party, and will act as a node through which to pass communication to party members or supporters.

The Fundraising Officer, or whoever is tasked with the success of the Merchandise Office, must be aware of several things. They must be aware of the cost of producing merchandise at various quantities. They must be aware of the profit margins of the various items and how many of each could expect to be sold in a certain time frame. They must be aware of the stocks of merchandise held by either the party or by party officials. Most importantly, they must be aware of how much money the Merchandise Office expects to return to the party. They must also be able to respond to any request for information from the Treasurer regarding inventory, expenses and income.

Having produced merchandise, the remaining work involves storing it and delivering it to the buyers. Anyone with a spare room or a decent garage will have enough room for a merchandise office that will be suitable for at least the party's initial requirements. If that person also has a reason to make frequent trips to the post office they can also post any merchandise that has been ordered.

A Basic Merchandise Office

Pens can be printed in party colours and with the party logo and/or website address. If it is too expensive to get pens printed in red, gold and green bands, three separate runs can be made, one for each colour. People will pay two dollars for a fifty cent pen, so this affords one of the largest profit margins of most items. Because of this, it is possible to give large discounts for bulk purchases and still turn a good profit.

T-shirts can be printed in a variety of sizes, colours and designs. If ordering a big run of t-shirts, keep in mind that people are getting larger faster than sizes are, and so it might be easier to sell 2XL and even 3XL than S. As for colours, almost anything is possible but black or white printed with the party logo will be the cheapest. T-shirts can easily be printed with a variety of designs, and someone in the movement will have some design talent. If five hundred t-shirts are to be printed, then five hundred dollars can be offered as a prize for the best design, and the cost of this will be a dollar per shirt.

Cigarette lighters are for obvious reasons a popular merchandise item, but as there are restrictions on posting them it might be best to focus on selling them at meetings and events. This postal restriction can be turned to the advantage of the movement. Print up a batch of lighters for every occasion that the party meets or performs any unified action. In this way they serve as a kind of memorabilia and carry a value that could not be achieved if they were sold to anyone.

If there is any musical talent in the movement, there is a very large profit margin on CDs and downloadable songs once the production costs have been recovered. Local artists might be willing to donate a track to the cause in exchange for publicity, and there are easily enough cannabis related songs out there to put together an album. A member with musical appreciation can order the songs in the way that sounds best, and copies can be made for a few dollars and sold for twenty.

Of course, anything that can have a logo slapped on it can potentially be merchandise. The Merchandise Office can move keyrings, mousepads, hoodies, drinking mugs, backpacks, USB sticks and much more from a range of online suppliers, most of whom only need an image of the logo.

A final idea is for the party to sell its own propaganda. This will require co-operation between the Information and Merchandise Officers. All the Information Officer has to do is supply a number of print-ready files for the Merchandise Officer to print in bulk. If the Merchandise Officer handles at least some of the distribution of propaganda, they can send it out when they complete merchandise orders.

Cannabonds

A cannabis law reform party, as a central node in the cannabis culture, can easily sell cannabonds to its supporters. A cannabond is a certificate that is bought with cash and can be exchanged for cannabis when it becomes legal to do so. Like other donations, it ought to be handled by the party Treasurer. It might even be worthwhile to make it known that cannabonds can only be purchased through the party Treasurer in order to prevent counterfeit.

If the party has contacts with a suitable artist (and this is very likely in a cannabis movement), they can be commissioned to produce an attractive certificate. The certificate ought to have a unique serial number in order to prevent counterfeit, and perhaps a seal, stamp, watermark or signature.

The beauty of cannabonds is that the party gets the cash immediately, and need only repay the bond once cannabis is legalised. When this happens, the party will be awash with cannabis anyway and will have no difficulty honouring the bonds.

Donations

Donations are almost pure profit. In many cases, nothing is expected in return for a donation, and when something is it is usually intangible, such as influence.

With a donation system, two elements are crucial. Firstly, the money must end up where it is best used. Secondly, the donation system must be as transparent as possible so that the maximum number of people are persuaded to donate the maximum amount of money.

Regarding the first element, a system must be in place so that the donation is overseen by the relevant Treasurer. If money is donated to a branch, the branch Treasurer must insure that it is accounted for and is spent wisely. The same is true for the party Treasurer. If the donation is made to a branch, it might be desirable for the national body to take a cut (unless the donation is made specifically for the operating expenses of that branch). Before any donations are taken in, the party should have a spending plan in place that ensures that the most important expenditures are accounted for first.

Regarding the second element, the donations process must be as transparent as possible. It is far easier to solicit a donation if the donor is told what the money will be used for and why having money to do this is necessary. If the donor wishes for some intangible return from their donation, it is essential that whoever takes in the donation has the authority to grant that request. For example, if someone wishes for a lunch with the party Leader in exchange for a sizeable donation, the Leader has to agree to this.

Targeting Groups or Individuals for Donations

One reason why it is important for the Membership Secretary to keep lists of supporters is because they are the same people who will provide much of the funding for the movement and must be contactable. The people who are most likely to make donations are those who have made donations in the past, provided it was not the recent past. The spare resources of the membership might not be enough to win anyway, so other avenues must be sought. The two obvious ones are individuals and corporations.

Individuals are often a good target for large donations because wealthy people are often more motivated by status than by more money. The historically successful model is that anyone with a good idea needs a patron in the form of someone with wealth.

Corporations will not be interested in much other than the profit potential, but this serves to simplify matters greatly. If anyone in the movement is able to analyse a marketplace, they could show the results of such an analysis to a company who could benefit from it. A textile company finding itself squeezed by lower labour costs in other countries might be very interested to hear of a market for high-end hemp clothing.

The next point involves who does the asking. Experience has shown that people are more likely to donate money if asked by the person who is running in the election than by someone working on behalf of that candidate.

Maximising Opportunities for Merchandising

In much the same way that people will not vote for the party if they are not aware of it, people will not buy party merchandise if they do not know it exists. There are many ways that a Fundraising Officer can bring attention to party merchandise, some of which require co-operation with other office holders and some which do not.

Once the Fundraising Officer is aware of what opportunities exist for merchandising and what the best price for each item is, they ought to put together a brochure in both printed and digital formats.

With a printed brochure, the Fundraising Officer needs to liaise with the Membership Secretary and any other party official tasked with posting correspondence to the membership. Because the Membership Secretary must, at a minimum, post a letter with a membership card and a welcome letter to each new member, they can easily slip in a merchandise brochure. New members will be excited to receive a membership pack and if they receive a merchandise brochure at the same time they will be inclined to buy. If another party official is tasked with sending letters to the membership, whether they be regular newsletters or special letters from the Leader, they can also add a merchandise brochure.

With a digital brochure, the Fundraising Officer needs to liaise with the Webmaster. Because the Internet allows the Webmaster to replicate information at almost no cost this is an excellent way of raising awareness. If the party website prominently displays merchandise offers, these will be seen by not only party members seeking updates but also by supporters who might be willing to buy merchandise even if they are unwilling to join the party. The digital nature of the party website means that it is easy to add new items or to offer special deals on old ones.

Although it requires far more work than any other merchandise item, the Fundraising Officer ought to work towards putting together a policy handbook for sale. The ideal way to do this is to recruit input from the various spokespeople in every policy area.

Merchandise and Memberships

One of the best avenues for selling merchandise is to do it at the same time as taking a membership application. Anyone willing to join the party will be on a high of enthusiasm and at this time they are more likely to also buy merchandise. A standard sheet of paper folded into thirds will have six panels, and if four are used for propaganda, one for the membership and one for the merchandise, it is possible to persuade a person to both become active and to buy things.

A more elegant method of achieving the same thing is to offer a range of premium memberships that come with discounted merchandise. Twenty, fifty and a hundred dollars are round numbers that would all ensure that the member gets a discount and the party gets some money.

A positive feedback loop should arise from these two departments: with revenue from memberships the party can get merchandise which can be offered with better memberships, the revenue from which can make even better merchandise.

Advertising

As soon as any communications channel has been opened up, it becomes possible for the operators of it to raise money by selling advertising. Although care has to be taken that the audience is not driven away by aggressive ads, people are so used to seeing advertising that small amounts of it will not raise any ire.

There are many ways of selling advertising, but the basic rules are the same. A company selling a good or a service pays the movement money to display ads on their communications channel. Whether the channel is a website, a newspaper or a magazine, it will have space that can be filled with an ad.

If the channel is well-known, advertisers might contact the party, otherwise the party (or its Fundraising Officer) will have to contact them. Any store that makes a considerable income from selling hydroponic equipment is a good bet, as are Internet headshops and bookstores. Take care not to advertise anything illegal - the prohibitionists will fall over themselves to shut a channel down if they have any justification at all.

Take caution with ad display programs such as Google AdSense. Some of them prohibit display on cannabis related websites and there is no sense in using ad space in this manner if the account gets banned upon the first human review.

A final point on advertising is that any properly equipped Merchandise Office ought to be able to advertise its wares through the party website. This means that the party can still make money even without selling its advertising space to a second party.

Money Raises the Stakes

The nature of cannabis law reform efforts changes considerably once money is added to the equation. No one in the party has the right to decide over how volunteer resources are used, but everyone will want a say in how money is spent, especially when an election is close.

It is absolutely crucial that money is prioritised. The party might have to pay a certain fee in order to contest an election and to run candidates in particular areas. The party will also have to pay the expenses of the Membership Office. These two areas, as well as any other area necessary for the survival of the party and its ability to contest elections, must receive funding before any other allocation is even considered.

Extra monies can be used in two ways. They can be saved for election expenses or they can be used to build the party. If the party is small and disorganised, the tendency will be to save everything for the election. The problem with this mentality is that, in the hands of a competent Fundraising Officer, extra money can be used to make more money. A run of a sufficient quantity of t-shirts, for example, can easily double the initial capital in a few months.

What is crucial is that the executive of the party agrees on how money is spent. Bickering over money can be time-consuming and wasteful. Usually the best time to come to an agreement is before the money is even made. A pragmatic solution might to be earmark a defined amount of future money for certain projects with the final decision on anything extra being made by the Treasurer. Another way is to agree that spending priority goes to whatever project will return the most money. In practice, this means that merchandising trumps media.

4. MEDIA

The purpose of media interaction is to inspire support for the movement. Media interaction has the advantage that a message can be given to a massive number of people, and it has the disadvantage that this message is relatively impersonal and usually unidirectional. Media interactions can be divided into events such as gatherings and protests, and media opportunities such as interviews, with the issuance of press releases falling somewhere in between.

Use An Events Calendar

The movement's website should have an events calendar. Many of the media opportunities outlined in this section will be events that will be planned months in advance. The most obvious date to put on the calendar is the date of the next election. Also important are dates of party events such as AGMs, or any other national, regional, branch or chapter meeting.

The rest of the calendar can be filled with any event that is of interest to people in cannabis law reform. If a prominent activist has a court hearing at a known date in the future, this should be in the calendar. If a roadshow, protest, gathering or speaking tour is planned, every date should be in the calendar. Any time a cannabis related bill is voted on, this should be in the calendar.

With this done, the events calendar itself becomes a crucial tool for building enthusiasm and momentum. If an important date is added, this can be followed up with an email to all members informing them of the date and its place in the events calendar. If the events calendar works as it should, an event need only be posted there and the party machine will ensure that it is a success.

It is also important that any person tasked with organising an event has their contact details available as part of the event entry.

Gatherings, Protests and Events

With a movement structure in place, gatherings such as protests and events can be held. An event such as a J Day serves several crucial purposes. It allows members to network by meeting a large number of like-minded people. It gives members a sense of legitimacy to see so many others who are inspired by the same cause. It gives the movement an excellent opportunity to attract new members and to fundraise. It gives both members and the wider public an opportunity to see the movement in action. It provides media opportunities. Perhaps most important of all, it inspires those who take part to do what it takes to achieve cannabis law reform. Each of these points are worth looking at in turn.

Because cannabis is illegal, it restricts social opportunities for those who use it. Holding a gathering allows people from a wide area to travel and to share and discuss ideas. It gives activists a chance to get to know higher-ups in the movement, and to challenge and develop trust with them. Activists can meet people from their area, which is crucial to developing and strengthening the branch structure of the movement. Gatherings allow people to learn, discuss and improve party policy.

Again because cannabis is illegal, a gathering imparts a sense of legitimacy to the cause. To have a hundred people meet in the same place will persuade those involved that the issue is large enough to be worth fighting for and to have a chance of success. With enough people, activists can assert their right to use cannabis even if this is in a public place.

Gatherings are the best times to sign up new members and to fundraise, and ideally the movement would ensure a table devoted to each. They attract large numbers of people who are not formally part of the movement, and many of these people might be inspired to join when they see the support of others. Activists often bring along sceptical friends who can be turned onto the cause when they hear about it from other activists. It is essential that a party official tasked with recruitment be present at gatherings. For social reasons, gatherings are the best time to sell merchandise. If an activist wears a t-shirt promoting the movement at a gathering, others will see it and will want one. Gatherings give party officials tasked with selling merchandise access to their ideal market. Also for social reasons, gatherings are the best time to solicit donations. Simply keeping a donations jar at either the membership or merchandise tables can bring in considerable money.

If the gathering is public, both members and the general populace will get a chance to see the movement in action. Members will see that the party infrastructure is capable of meaningful action, and people not affiliated with the movement might be surprised at the level of support displayed. A large proportion of voters consider cannabis law reform a fringe issue, and to see several thousand activists gathering in support of it will make them reconsider this opinion.

Gatherings are excellent media opportunities. At the very least, websites that support the movement must be able to generate or take possession of images and reports. The movement infrastructure must ensure that someone is responsible for taking photos of the gathering and for writing a report on how it went. No matter where in the country a supporter is, to see photos of thousands of people smoking cannabis in a public park will inspire them. The party Media Team should work to ensure coverage from local or national newspapers, television or radio stations. In many cases journalists will wish to speak to party officials - the Media Team must ensure that this is facilitated and that the journalist receives as much information as they need.

Any and all of these factors serve to inspire people to work towards cannabis law reform. Party leaders can take the opportunity to deliver a speech to a receptive audience.

Cannabis Tours and Roadshows

If the movement has sufficient funds, it can organise a cannabis roadshow to take the message across the country. A cannabis roadshow is a great way of building support, for some party officials to make themselves known to supporters and to the media, and to fundraise.

Before a roadshow can begin to be planned, it must be

made clear how much money is available for expenses. Although donations can and should be solicited along the way, it is good to know how much of a lump sum is available so that the roadshow does not start out desperate for cash.

Once this is determined, the organisers can plan the number of stops, how much time shall be spent at each stop, where the roadshow staff will set up, what information they will display and how it will be displayed.

The number of stops and the amount of time spent at each stop is primarily a function of how much support the roadshow staff can expect at each location. For this reason it is crucial that one of the roadshow organisers is the Membership Secretary. The Membership Secretary will know how many members of the movement are present in each location, how active they are, and how or whether they can be contacted to inform them of the roadshow. The idea is that the roadshow staff will be met at each stop by members of the movement, by anyone these members can bring along as well as by any member of the public that might be interested. Ideally, the roadshow ought to make as many stops as possible and spend a couple of days at each stop if there is sufficient possibility of support there. Many members of the movement will be happy to provide accommodation for the roadshow staff, especially if the staff are party officials who are known to those members.

The next step is to determine where the roadshow will set up in each location. This might depend on the logistical capacity of the roadshow team. Although it is best, if numbers permit, to hire a hall of some kind, there may not be enough support or money to do this. The roadshow can always set up at the side of a busy thoroughfare for foot traffic if permission can be secured. Outside a shopping mall or at a square in the centre of the city are good targets. It is best to have a backup location as well, should rain or hostile forces prevent the roadshow from setting up in the most desirable location. It is a good idea here to draw on the knowledge of local members for advice on where to set up.

The decision as to what information to display and how it shall be displayed is a decision that the roadshow organisers should come to in consultation with the Information Officer. The main consideration is to assemble a dozen or so freestanding boards to which A0-sized posters can be stapled. Each of these posters should cover one major area of cannabis law reform, with a striking title and font large enough so that a person walking past could read it. The purpose of these information boards is that, when there are too many people for the staff to speak to individually, interested parties can still get information.

Related to this is the choice of what information to hand out. This is one area in which the roadshow format excels. If the roadshow has a decent sized vehicle it can carry boxes of photocopied pamphlets on any number of cannabis related topics. These can then be handed out at the slightest expression of interest.

Two other crucial elements of a successful roadshow are a merchandise table and a recruitment desk. If space or staffing does not permit two, they can be combined into a single table. Many of the people who come to a roadshow stop will not have heard the argument for cannabis law reform before, or at least will not have heard it put so persuasively. For this reason it is important that the opportunity is offered to join the movement, or at least to take away one or several membership forms. Because many of the people present will be supporters or even members, a roadshow offers an excellent opportunity to buy merchandise without paying for postage. Having a donations jar at the desk is important as well.

The Press Secretary can also get involved in a roadshow by contacting media outlets in advance and alerting them to its presence. Even better would be to organise interviews at as many stops as possible.

On the subject of who should go on a roadshow, the movement needs to decide who will best achieve its objectives. At a minimum it is desirable to have one person who is comfortable speaking to crowds and one person who is articulate, inspiring and persuasive on a person-to-person level. The roadshow need not have the same people throughout, although if it does it will be easier to organise.

Concerts

Another good idea to raise the profile of the movement is to throw a concert. Most cannabis users are also music lovers and many of them are skilled musicians themselves. Organising a concert is simpler than organising a roadshow and more exciting.

The first thing that needs to be done is to line up a venue. With a venue sorted, the organisers can try and find some bands. The right band is one whose lyrics or sound carries the cannabis law reform message. Then the organiser can work on promotion.

Just as with roadshows, it is important that the concert organiser offers a chance for concertgoers to join the party and to buy merchandise. People are already used to the idea of buying t-shirts at concerts so any merchandise table should be stocked with a good supply of those. If a party official can be tasked with recruitment they can join the table for that reason.

Press Releases

The issuance of press releases is a core activity and responsibility of the Press Secretary at every stage of the electoral cycle. Because of this it is crucial that the Press Secretary has an excellent grasp of English and of party policy.

There is almost no limit to the range of subjects that a press release could cover. The most important consideration is that the press release points out a problem or inefficiency in the current political system that the cannabis law reform party could improve upon if it was voted into power.

If there is a news report that demonstrates that police resources are insufficient (such as if an investigation was bungled or if a crime was reported and no police officer could get to the scene in time), then the cannabis law reform party could issue a press release pointing out how much money a repeal of cannabis prohibition could save, and how these savings could be used to make the police force more effective.

Whenever a person is penalised harshly because of cannabis prohibition (if they receive a lengthy prison sentence or if their assets are seized), a press release can point this out. Any time that an elderly citizen or a young adult with a family is arrested, a press release can summon support and outrage.

When the party becomes larger and there are individuals who can fill the roles of spokespeople for particular policy areas, it becomes possible to generate a large number of press releases in a short time. Any news report that mentions a certain policy area could potentially inspire a press release.

Press releases need not be solely reactive. If the party achieves a certain number of members, or if there is a change in a senior leadership position, then a press release can be issued.

In order to get the press release out to where it could be picked up by a media outlet, the Press Secretary needs to have a list that includes a contact person at as many different outlets as possible, both national and local, and for all different media. It is a good idea to ensure that the Press Secretary is the one tasked with doing this, because then they can check the accuracy and quality of the press release before it is issued. It is essential for the party image that the text of the press release contains no spelling or grammatical errors, or factual inaccuracies.

Letters to Representatives

Letters to politicians are a form of media, because they do get the message of the movement out to a person who can potentially do something about it. Cynics might believe that such letters are of little use if they are not sent in an envelope that contains a thick wad of cash. Indeed, there are no examples of politicians receiving correspondence from cannabis law reform activists and launching a campaign to end prohibition.

Nonetheless, there is still reason to send letters to politicians, especially if any kind of response can be elicited. The reason for this is because once the position of any politician on the legalisation spectrum is known, that politician can be influenced to vote for legislation that promotes cannabis law reform.

If the politician is strongly against cannabis law reform, and has gone on the record as such, then they can be publicly blamed for the negative effects of prohibition. If there is a family who has lost a provider, or a patient who cannot get the right medicine, and if these victims wish to appear in front of the media, they can damage the image of the politician as long as that politician continues to espouse prohibition.

Likewise, if the politician is in favour of law reform, create a channel through which this can be known to people in the movement. If the movement has a newsletter, it can be mentioned that certain politicians are, to some degree at least, behind the cause. Care must be taken not to give these politicians so much publicity that they take support away from the candidates of the cannabis law reform party.

With the positions of politicians established, cannabis law reform activists can write further letters in an ongoing attempt to make the case. Activists can tell the politicians directly that the activist puts heavy weight on the politician's position on cannabis law reform when deciding who to vote for. This is a classic example of an action which is exponentially effective when large numbers of people take part.

The Party Website

Over and above the opportunities for organising the movement, the website of any cannabis law reform party is one of the best ways to get content out to people for little cost in either time or money. Although the Webmaster ought to build forums that are mostly accessible only to members, a website can transmit information to a large number of people who are not formally part of the movement. Any supporter who is concerned about their name getting out in connection to cannabis (and there will be large numbers of these) can still go to the website as often as it is updated. This section looks at what should go on the party website.

The most obvious way to use the website's front page is to draw attention to exposure in other media forms. If a party member is interviewed or featured in a blog, put a link up on the website. Likewise with radio, television (where possible) or any form of social media. Executive members can write posts on new merchandise or new policy announcements, and other members can draw attention to what is happening in their area.

There is always something happening with cannabis law reform somewhere in the world, so if the Webmaster keeps aware of events they can notify people in their area through the website. Because many countries are currently experimenting with some relaxation of the cannabis laws there are a large number of posts on other blogs with announcements of law changes and reports of the effects of these changes.

If there is a party member who keeps up with recent psychological or medical research they will read a number of cannabis related stories in trade publications. If these are online they can be linked to from the front page and even if they are not they can be summarised with a reference to the printed work given.

It is also easy, if the website is built with the right content management system, to download and install a plugin that displays a news feed of cannabis related topics. If this is customised to the area in which the party operates then people can get a stream of cannabis news with almost no effort on the part of the Webmaster.

Media Opportunities

Media opportunities are high stakes events, and for this reason it is crucial that they are handled correctly. Seeing a party official on television or reading about an activist in a newspaper might be the first impression that many people have of the movement, and if a sufficient impression is made the media consumer might choose to vote for the party or to take their interest further.

The court of public opinion has fewer rules than an

ordinary courtroom. In many cases, the cannabis law reform movement has already been tried in the court of public opinion. Cannabis users are frequently seen as stupid, lazy, dishonest, arrogant and naive, if not outright vicious criminals. Any media opportunity will give party officials a chance to counter these stereotypes as well as put forward the argument for cannabis law reform.

The remainder of this section examines the various media opportunities that a cannabis law reform movement can take advantage of and the considerations that are involved.

Print Media

There are two basic ways to gain attention for cannabis law reform through print media: interviews and letters to the opinion pages of newspapers.

Arranging an interview can occur in one of two ways. Either a journalist contacts the party because they wish to feature a party official or the party Press Secretary contacts a journalist to inform them of an interesting event. A journalist might contact the party at any time, especially if there is an election looming. The higher the profile of the movement the more likely it is that a journalist will contact the party; if the party has established itself as an authority on the cannabis issue, this may occur whenever cannabis law reform is raised in the public consciousness or when there is a noteworthy cannabis related trial. The other option is for the party Press Secretary to contact a journalist, which could happen in conjunction with a roadshow, a protest, a concert or at any other time when the cannabis issue gains attention.

Letters to the opinion pages are excellent because they reach a wide range of people and many of those who do read them are politically active. Because people who read newspapers almost always vote there is high potential for return on investment. The top prize for the movement is to get an editorial arguing the case for cannabis law reform in a major newspaper. If this is achieved the chances are good that letters in response to this will be prominent over coming weeks, which will keep the cannabis issue in the public mind. Letters to the editor are not as good but they are nonetheless very effective. Anyone who chooses to write one should be aware that there will be a word limit and exceeding it may ensure the letter does not get printed or becomes abridged in a way that limits or even damages the message.

On the choice of topic for a letter, any argument given in Part Two of this handbook ("A Discussion of Cannabis Law Reform Related Arguments") can be rewritten and submitted. It is best if the letter is sent in response to a cannabis-related item that was published in the newspaper in recent days. For example, if it is reported that local police spent $2,000,000 on a large cannabis bust, it can be pointed out that this money would have been much better spent on policing crimes of sex or violence.

An excellent example of a sustained letter-writing campaign is that carried out by Steven Wilkinson of the Aotearoa Legalise Cannabis Party. Any activist looking for tips can visit the ALCP website at www.alcp.org.nz

and find the Letters to Editor subforum, where hundreds of Steven's letters have been reposted.

Letters to the editor do not have to go through the party Press Secretary. Because they are not official party statements the Press Secretary cannot enforce them anyway, but if people in the movement intend to write them it is a good idea for them to do it correctly. Correct spelling and grammar is vital, as is stating only correct facts and not using fallacious reasoning. The idea is to put the argument for cannabis law reform across in a polite, intelligent, respectful and civil way.

If the party is organised, a group of members can work to support each other. A letter to the editor is far more likely to raise public awareness if it is followed up with another letter by another person, who can either support the original letter, provide rebuttal to its detractors or develop points independently.

Although it is tempting, the movement must not provide template letters with the intent of individual activists signing them and sending these to their local newspaper. The same company might own many newspapers and that company might keep track of the content of letters to all of their outlets. If they believe that they are being spammed by cannabis activists they could blacklist the movement or even provide unhelpful coverage. Modifying the message is not difficult and if the letter is unique to the time and place it is published in it will be far more effective.

Radio

Although radio has, to a large extent, been replaced by television, it is still an effective way of getting a message to many people at once. Radio is like television and not like print media in the sense that time is far more limited. A print journalist can perform a lengthy interview and choose the best parts of it for a story; on the radio, the listeners hear whatever the interviewee says (and how they say it).

Because time is at a premium, the message will have to be concise and clear, and this means that the activist will have to consider their audience and tailor their message to suit. Student listeners might be excited to hear an activist talk about resisting oppressive and unjustified authority whereas a farmer listening to a broadcast as he fixes a fence might be more interested in the potential for hemp farming. Because a large number of elderly people prefer the radio to any other medium it is a good idea to target them with arguments for medical marijuana. It is also an advantage to know in advance how much time is allocated for the interview. If there is a specific point that the listeners ought to take away, this can be repeated or stated with special emphasis.

How the message is put across is just as important as what the message is. Radio might be an auditory medium, but the listener will often form a visual image of what is being said as they hear it. Part of this image will involve the speaker's personality and body language. The activist should speak warmly and with passion, as if they are giving a wedding speech. They should take care to be sitting upright when speaking or even standing if possible, as this will allow the voice to carry in a more relaxed and resonant manner. They should also speak slowly, not so slowly that they appear to think they're speaking to idiots but not much quicker than that.

One advantage that radio has is that there are thousands of radio shows with different themes. Any of them dedicated to reggae, to politics or, ideally, to cannabis culture, might be willing to let a cannabis law reform activist speak at length about their mission. Student radio also reaches out to an audience likely to be sympathetic to cannabis law reform.

A final point is that radio is unlike both print and television media in that listeners are most likely to be doing something else as they listen. They might be in their car, doing yardwork or on the shop floor. If the listener's attention is divided the activist will have to speak in a more arresting fashion if they want to make an impression.

Talkback Radio

Talkback radio is sometimes one of the best democratic platforms. Even without a scheduled interview, a cannabis law reform activist can bring a message to thousands of people in a few seconds. The activist need not make a call with the intent of specifically arguing for cannabis law reform, and talkback radio hosts are not fond of political fanatics ranting over their airwaves (unless it is them).

There are two ways of subtly raising the issue. One is to

talk about a related issue and the other is to raise a problem and then offer cannabis law reform as a solution. Both methods will work better if the issue is framed in economic terms, because this will appeal to a large number of people and the economy is usually one of the foremost issues on any given day.

An example of the first method is to call in and complain about the cost of incarcerating non-violent offenders, and hoping for the issue of cannabis law reform to be raised indirectly. An example of the second is to call in and mention the ease with which teenagers are buying cannabis, with a view to later offering regulation as a solution.

Another advantage of talkback radio is that it offers excellent practice for the media pressures any candidate will face during a campaign. The activist must sit in silence until they are suddenly on air and speaking to an audience, and then they are moderated by an easily bored and often rude host who might have a reputation for abusing his guests.

Television

For a cannabis law reform movement in most modern Western nations, a slot on television is the ultimate prize. No other medium will give the movement a greater opportunity to impart information. Unlike the other media, television gives potential voters and supporters an opportunity to measure the appearance and body language of party officials.

If the membership is fighting a ground war and the

media is the air force, the television is the nuke. It is the gamebreaker. Many a politician has been rescued from electoral oblivion thanks to a ten second comment at the right place and time, and many a frontrunner has been destroyed by the converse.

It is unlikely that a cannabis law reform movement will get anyone other than its leader onto the national stage at one time. It is not necessary to.

What is crucial with any television appearance is that the representative is visually presentable, and that their message comes across clearly and with confidence. To succeed in this second regard means that the party representative must have spent considerable time practising their approach. Mock interviews conducted in front of other party members or in front of the mirror will make sure that the representative appears calm and collected.

Online Media

In much the same way that the party can be organised far more effectively if it uses the Internet, the party can promote itself far more effectively using this medium. Online media replicates all the advantages of print, radio and television media as well as offering promotion through social media. This section will look at all four in turn.

A static blog is the online equivalent of a newspaper. It is easier to feature in a blog for the reason that it is usually smaller than a newspaper and more desperate for content. The best course of action is to find a blog that solicits guest posts and offer to write one for them on the subject of cannabis law reform. This offers most of the advantages of a newspaper editorial, with a significant bonus: viewers can leave comments, which often gets a good discussion going. As with letters to the editor, an activist can rewrite one or several of the arguments from Part Two of this handbook, with their own spin to make it relevant to the time and place.

Streaming audio and podcasts are the equivalent of radio. Many radio stations will stream part or all of their radio broadcast, and if an activist or party official can get an interview they have the opportunity to reach a large number of people. Other websites might offer podcasts to their visitors. A podcast is nothing more than a large audio file that represents an "episode" of the broadcast. Some cannabis related websites will make podcasts of interviews with cannabis law reform activists and post them for free. The movement does not have to wait to be interviewed, however: it can use its own website to disseminate podcasts that its members have recorded themselves.

Television media is replicated by video sharing sites, of which the best known is YouTube. These sites are a fantastic way to get a message across to people who are used to watching television. With any modern digital camera, an activist can record themselves speaking on a cannabis related subject and post it to YouTube. If they have some video editing software, it can be a good idea to edit the video to show a still screen with text that asks a particular question about cannabis law reform, which the activist then answers. If an election is approaching, it is a good idea for every candidate and member of the party executive to post a video in which they discuss their plans and hopes for their constituency and for the nation. Apart from monologues, videos of cannabis action such as public speeches or gatherings can inspire people to take up and support the message. Links to all of these videos can be posted to the party website.

No complete examination of online media is possible without a discussion of social media, such as Facebook or Twitter. Any media event, whether it be a protest, gathering, roadshow, concert or interview, can be shared on any activist's Facebook page. If a decent proportion of activists use Facebook to promote the party message, thousands or even tens of thousands of people can become aware of any cannabis action within hours.

The Party Newsletter or Magazine

For any party to succeed, it has to develop a culture, and one way of developing a party culture is to have a newsletter that is exclusive to members. It may not be economical to post a regular newsletter out to all members, but in this age most members will volunteer an email address. A basic Word or Open Office document can export a .pdf which can then be sent as an attachment to the emails of the party membership.

The newsletter should inform the membership of any possibility they might have to get involved with the success of the movement, whether they realise it or not. It can also contain communication to them by members of the Executive, reminders of their rights and even recipes.

If the party elects a Newsletter Editor then they have a media position on the same order as the Webmaster. The degree to which this is feasible is a direct function of the size of the party. With a big enough party, the Newsletter Editor can solicit enough quality contributions to produce an engaging document. The greater the membership, the more pages can be produced, which means more advertising revenue can be gathered.

As with the party website, the most important element of the newsletter is the content. The main difference is that, because the newsletter only goes out to members, it can be a bit more intimate. This makes it the best place to tell the personal story of any of the members who may wish this be done.

The personal stories of activists are always interesting. When did an activist realise that prohibition was bullshit? What was their first action? What do they think is the best way to win? Telling the story of an activist both inspires members to become more active and builds solidarity as members realise that they have more in common with the people fighting for their cause.

The personal stories of people whose lives have been ruined by prohibition are also interesting. While care has to be taken not to turn the party newsletter into a platform for hand-wringing, the occasional case study of a true victim of prohibition will easily find a readership. Truly inhumane cases might generate enough outrage to become active movements in their own right.

Martyrs

Every rights movement will have its martyrs. Sooner or later there will be a peaceful cannabis smoker who is brutalised by the police, or a heavily sick person who is sentenced to prison because they used cannabis as a medicine. If this person wishes to use their own experience to expose the cruelty of cannabis prohibition, then the movement must recognise this as a win/win situation.

The party Press Secretary needs to take the initiative if a case like this comes to their attention. If the Press Secretary knows a sympathetic journalist in the same region as the martyr, an introduction could be made that leads to the story becoming public. In any case, the Press Secretary can at least arrange for the martyr's story to be told on the party website or YouTube channel.

Should the movement wish to create a small buzz, they can run a competition where victims of cannabis prohibition tell their story, whether in text or on video. Stories can be published in the party newsletter, and videos can be added to the party YouTube channel. Whoever has the best story or video can win a sum of money, or goods equal to this value.

The Media Does Not Hate You

A cognitive bias that often afflicts people who believe strongly in a political cause is the hostile media effect. Sometimes this is because the media is reinforcing a worldview that is hostile to supporters of a certain cause, and sometimes it is because the moral values of the supporters are so far away from the average person's that a perfectly objective publication will still be seen as disagreeable.

The truth is that the national political media is usually concerned with the social democrats, with the conservatives and with foreign affairs. It has not been common for a cannabis law reform movement to get onto the national agenda in the past. This is not because the media is hostile but because the cannabis issue will never trump issues of war and peace in the national consciousness. A cannabis law reform activist might get on the primetime news, but they would be lucky to get more than a few seconds of exposure.

For this reason, local media is often a better target. Unless the cannabis law reform movement can get a hundred thousand people into the streets, the local media is likely to provide a more realistic avenue for mass attention. This can sometimes happen if the local media find out about a human interest story that might be of interest to their audience.

What must be avoided is for any member to take on an antagonistic approach to the media. If the media ignores a candidate or does not print a letter, this is probably because they have decided that there is something more interesting on. It is not past of a vast conspiracy intended to deny the cannabis law reform movement their time in the sun. If the media can be given a reason to care, they will start caring, and they will care most about what will help them sell the advertising that is their main revenue stream. If an activist comes out and accuses the media of corruption and bias, that candidate will be suffocated with silence.

Some Notes on Viral Marketing

The idea of viral marketing is that awareness of a subject or product increases exponentially and achieves saturation within a short period of time. The fact that there are far more avenues available to the modern marketer means that there is a much better chance of something going viral in the public consciousness. Someone might read about a story on the party website, tell their friends at work the next day, who all link to the story on their Facebook pages, where all their friends read it. If a story is deemed interesting enough it can spread very fast in this manner.

There are really two marketing approaches: to go wide or to go deep. To go wide means to reach out to as many people as possible, and to go deep means to heavily influence those people that are reached. Ideally a marketer would like to do both, and anyone putting together a cannabis law reform movement must believe that they will succeed if only they could get enough people on board.

If a message goes wide on a medium such as Facebook or Twitter, and if it includes an avenue through which people can come back to the party webpage, it can also go deep. The party website should be comprehensive enough so that anyone who is interested in cannabis law reform can read about an area of it that they find interesting enough to share with someone else. Unless the party controls a media machine it is hard to know in advance which issue has the best chance of making an impact; it is best, therefore, to develop the website as far as possible.

Use Media in Synergy

If an activist uses a form of media to get the attention of even one person, it is important that that person be told where they can access further media should they wish to. The easiest way to do this is to make a reference to the party website, because if a person knows the party URL they can find out almost anything else they need to know about party organisation or policy.

The other way to do this is to ensure that, wherever possible, media created by the party for informational purposes offers merchandise for sale. If it costs ten cents to print a pamphlet, and that pamphlet offers information and propaganda as well as the opportunity to buy a t-shirt for twenty dollars of which ten is profit, then a purchase rate of one percent or better will allow all of the pamphlets to be funded by t-shirt sales.

Cannabis Terminology and Etiquette

No matter which medium is used, when arguing for cannabis law reform it is important to be precise, to be clearly understood and to be persuasive. In achieving any of these things it is necessary to use the correct terminology. Cannabis terminology is often vague and inaccurate for the reason that prohibitionists have appropriated words and have framed the cannabis debate in certain terms. Being correct in this regard will make the message clearer and will open people's minds to be more receptive of it.

Never use the phrase "alcohol and drugs." Not only is this phrase redundant (alcohol is, of course, a drug), but it is a stock phrase of the establishment when it wishes to paint cannabis as if it belongs in in a different, more dangerous, class to alcohol. If this phrase is used by a second party in conversation, an activist should point out that it is inaccurate and even stupid.

Likewise, try not to use the term "marijuana." Although many activists use it as part of the phrase "medical marijuana", this is only for the alliteration effect and it is otherwise generally avoided. This is because, in the early days of prohibition, cannabis opponents focused the public attention on "marijuana" so as to associate it with the Mexican manual labourers who were feared and despised by much of the population (or, at least, the elements of it receptive to arguments for cannabis prohibition). "Cannabis" is the scientific term for the plant and as such carries much less in the way of connotation.

Having said this, it is foolish to get too hung up on what words may be used and which may not. In any cannabis law reform movement there will be people who identify with certain terms and other who see them as pejorative. The best rule is to let it slide: we are fighting a civil rights war and telling people how to speak their own language will not help. The prohibitionists would love to see cannabis law reform activists argue over whether cannabis users should be called "stoners" or not, and every hour spent arguing about it is an hour less spent on recruitment and fundraising.

Likewise, no-one wins from rigidly enforced rules of

118

etiquette that go beyond conventional social norms such as no stealing, killing etc. Many a chapter has been destroyed by some blowhard getting on their high horse about whether joints are passed to the left or to the right. Let it slide. Always keep in mind that every argument within the cannabis law reform movement is paid for in solidarity.

PART TWO: A DISCUSSION OF CANNABIS LAW REFORM RELATED ARGUMENTS

The art of winning votes is nothing more than applied psychology. There is enough material about psychology to fill several libraries, but some of it is more crucial than others and will be discussed here. This part of the book describes how action continues once the structure of the movement has been created.

The focus of this part of the book is on the multitudes of one-on-one contact sessions that activists will inevitably have with neutrals or supporters in order to get them to become more active. The movement can only be a success if it uses the infrastructure described in the first part of this book to persuade individuals to vote for cannabis law reform. As other political movements have shown, elections are won person by person, much as wars are won yard by yard.

This part of the book discusses what activists need to consider once they have made the decision to raise the profile and support of the party to the point where it is rewarded by voters. A thorough understanding of this section also has the potential to make any action taken in the media much more effective.

The Purpose of Arguing in Favour of Cannabis Law Reform

In accordance with the objectives of any cannabis law reform movement, the purpose of making a case for cannabis law reform is to gain support for it. This might have the intended effect of making a member into an activist, a supporter into a member, or a neutral party into a supporter. The core principle here is that any action that raises support for the movement will gradually move the party into a place where it can win (or at least achieve its objectives in) an election.

Because humans think, and because much of this thought occurs below a conscious level, there are essentially three ways that support can be raised. A person can be informed of something they didn't know, or they can be informed that something they thought they knew is false, or they can be so impressed by the activist that they elect to support them without necessarily being intellectually persuaded.

If an election is far away, it is relatively more important to convert members to activists. The earlier this is done the more time the activist will have to put systems into place, and because work done by activists tends to have an exponential effect, it will become more effective the earlier it is started. If an election is close, it is relatively more important to convert neutrals to supporters (assuming that supporters will vote). This is because little can be done to make people into effective activists if an election is close and a vote is still much better than nothing.

The simple rule is: persuade people to be as active as possible, and do this as early as possible.

The Basics of the Psychology of Persuasion

Activists must never forget that, when arguing the case for cannabis law reform, their objective is to attract votes. It is not to defeat the case of the prohibitionists. It is not to espouse the wonders of cannabis. It is not to abuse the politicians, police or business interests. It may not even be necessary to tell the truth (this is discussed in detail below).

The truth is that a person's decision on whom to vote for is dependent on a far broader range of factors than the intellectual arguments behind that party and its policies. Ultimately, in order to persuade someone to vote for the cannabis law reform party they must be convinced that it is in their personal benefit to do so. Even in cases where an argument for improving society through cannabis law reform is made, if society would not be improved in a way that accords with that person's own values they will not support it. It is important to remember that, as voting populations become wealthier, they vote less on their wallet and more on their values.

No matter how much a person can be convinced that it is their best interest to vote for cannabis law reform, casting a vote depends on more than this. It is taken for granted that readers of this handbook live in some kind of representative democracy. This means that people will vote for people like them, or at least people who they believe will care about them. This is the point at which image becomes crucial. If an activist destroys the case of the prohibitionists, but does so in a sneering and arrogant manner, they might lose votes. A person insecure about their educational level will not be impressed by a lengthy dissection of his government's behaviour as it relates to international law and the United Nations.

If an activist can present an argument that appeals to a person's better nature, and at the same time appear to be someone that that person would like to have a beer (or maybe a joint) with, then they will have an excellent chance of success. Even if these methods fail, most people can see the raw self-interest in some kind of cannabis law reform.

Intellectual versus Emotional Persuasion

People can be persuaded to support cannabis law reform through one of two means. They can be persuaded intellectually, with reference to research, facts and figures, or they can be persuaded emotionally. Each method has advantages and disadvantages, and a time and place.

The advantage with intellectual persuasion is that if you have a better case than the opposition, you will win. Compared to emotional persuasion, intellectual persuasion also has the advantage of being permanent. The major disadvantage is that intellectual persuasion is not very motivating. An activist can convince someone that there is a case for cannabis law reform - but so what? If the person being persuaded is not at least motivated to vote, the efforts are wasted. The other major disadvantage is that intellectual persuasion is slow. Someone might want to take time to consider the points an activist has made or to research them further, and this could take weeks, months or longer.

The advantage with emotional persuasion is that it is fast, and that it is motivating. A person subject to this will pay much closer attention to how the argument is made, rather than what the argument is. The crucial disadvantage is that it is volatile. If a person only agrees with the case for cannabis law reform if they are feeling a certain emotion, persuasion will only be effective as long as that emotion is maintained. Another disadvantage is that not all emotions can be manipulated. If a person is against cannabis law reform because they absolutely despise cannabis users, little can be done to turn them into a voter for cannabis law reform.

The general rule is, the further away an election, the greater the advantage in focusing on intellectual arguments. Someone persuaded by the intellectual arguments for reform is more likely to become a dependable, long-term agitator for change than someone who just gets fired up with no way of directing their anger (other than voting).

In practice, a concerted effort to persuade someone to support cannabis law reform will involve both intellectual and emotional arguments. In many cases, an activist must first win the intellectual argument and then appeal to emotions; there is little point in motivating someone to vote if they do not vote for you.

The Spectrum of Support and Persuasion Style

Arguing in favour of cannabis law reform will have objectives that are dependent on where the target already is on the spectrum of activists < members < supporters < neutrals.

Someone who is already an activist does not need to hear intellectual arguments for cannabis law reform (unless the idea is to suggest arguments that they can use themselves). They are already committed. Intellectual arguments will not shift them. What is crucial is that they are motivated to take action on behalf of the movement. To this end they should be targeted with emotional arguments.

Members and supporters of the movement are in similar categories, but are open to both forms of persuasion. They might not be activists because they are not completely convinced of the intellectual argument for reform. They might not be activists because they are insufficiently motivated.

Neutrals are in a different category. Arguments to their emotions might be seen as manipulative or dishonest. Emotional appeals to the damage caused to cannabis users might be ineffective for the simple reason that the neutral might not care about cannabis users. The range of neutrals is very broad. Some of them may be cannabis users who did not intend to vote for the party because they did not know that it existed. Some of them may actually despise cannabis users.

Once a person makes the decision to support the

cannabis law reform movement, a watershed is crossed. At this point, arguments to emotions will elicit more support than intellectual ones. The activist will have to judge when this point is reached, but it generally occurs when the person declares that they will vote for the party.

The Message Must be Tailored

What is central to any effort to gather support for cannabis law reform is that the arguments put forward for it are tailored to the audience. A struggling family of four might be very interested to hear that the savings from enacting cannabis law reform could be used to reduce taxes, especially if they are consumption taxes. Someone young and middle-class might be more interested in hearing that cannabis law reform is a good way of reducing government interference in people's lives, and a bikie might just want to give the middle finger to The Man.

Generally, the more individualistic a person is the more receptive they will be to arguments from economics, and the more social a person is the more receptive they will be to arguments from humanitarianism. Having said this, when it comes to cannabis law reform most people are receptive to both or neither. The latter two sections of this part of the book discuss individual arguments and the type of people who might be most influenced by them.

The Image Must be Tailored

Equally as important as the message is the image.

Subconsciously, every voter is aware that they live in a representative democracy and most will not choose to be represented by a hippie with a massive, unkempt beard and soup-stained clothing, no matter how eloquently he puts an argument forward. Although cannabis users are frequently negatively stereotyped, this can actually work to the activist's advantage if they can display an image that counters this, because once a person accepts that their stereotypes are not accurate they will naturally wonder where else they could have been wrong - and the activist is right there to tell them.

It is vital that party officers in the public eye appear unobjectionable to a majority of people. This does not mean that they must be cookie-cutter corporate clones with no personality, but if an activist presents themselves so that a neutral might have little concern about inviting the activist into their home, much of the battle is won in an instant. To this end it can be an advantage for party officials to appear in suits, with a formal shirt and a tie, and tidy shoes. It is also good to avoid obvious signs of a failure or disinclination to fit into society, like facial tattoos, missing front teeth or scraggly dirty hair. There will always be an element of "fuck the system" in any cannabis law reform movement but it should be remembered that promoting such an attitude aggressively will turn many people away.

If an activist is seeking representation in the legislative body, then they are effectively auditioning for a job. The basic rule here is to present themselves as they would for a job interview.

127

The Perception of Honesty

For a potential voter to be open to persuasion from a
cannabis law reform activist, the voter has to trust the
activist. If the voter believes or suspects that the activist
is lying, whether directly or by omission, no argument
can be successful. To achieve this, two ends must be
met.

The first and most obvious is that the activist must not
lie, at least not if there is any chance that the voter
knows it's a lie. If the voter knows the activist is not
telling the truth then this will send the movement
backwards. It must be emphasised here that it is the
perception of honesty which is important. The activist
should avoid making claims that sound untrue if these
cannot be proven - even if they are absolutely true.
Claiming that cannabis instantly cures cancer, that it is
the most wonderful plant of them all, that it is only
illegal due to a multigenerational conspiracy of
government, bankers, media, mental health workers,
industrialists and communists: none of this will persuade
the average voter to support cannabis law reform. At all
times it is best to stick to documented facts, and to give
any sceptics a source that they can research themselves.

The second and more difficult of the two is that the party
must get its facts straight before it can try to persuade
people. The party must at least agree on how many
cannabis users there are and how much money it costs
for the justice system to attack them. It does the
movement no good for one member to claim that there
are a hundred thousand cannabis users in a certain area
and for another to claim there are a million. In many

cases the government itself will have commissioned a recent drug survey that attempted to establish how many cannabis users there are in the country. If this is the case, data from this survey should be used.

The party's Information Officer should keep records of any statistic or fact that the party believes will be frequently used. They ought to find the most authoritative source they can, as long as this is not biased against the objectives of the movement, and make sure that all activists are aware of and reference this source. If the Ministry of Justice publishes official figures on how much it costs to incarcerate one prisoner for a year, make sure everyone knows it. If there are official figures on how many cannabis prisoners there are, make sure everyone knows that.

The Basics of Building a Rapport

Very few people form political opinions based on cold reason. If you can make a person think that you genuinely like them and care about them they will be far more receptive to your message. Crucial to achieving either is to make sure that the activist treats every person with respect. The younger the activist is, the more important it is that they do this, because people will be more sensitive to disrespect if they speak with someone younger than themselves.

If a person is voicing their misgivings with cannabis law reform or what they believe the effects of it will be, do not interrupt them. Even if they say their piece and walk off, this is preferable to escalating an argument into a dominance contest. Hear them out, and then respond in a way that makes it clear that you heard them: "It sounds like you have misgivings about X" is a great way to show that you have listened and that you have understood. If they then think their position is respected they will be far more likely to listen to and respect your counterargument.

When making a counterargument it is important to make clear that the listener is not made to feel that they formed their opinion because they were too stupid, ignorant, misguided or brainwashed to properly grasp the issue. If you make a claim based on figures, use recent figures so as to imply that most people are not aware of the truth. If you want to refer to the effects of some cannabis law reform policy elsewhere in the world, say "Many people don't know that X." If someone comes up with a bad idea, say "That has been suggested in the past, and the problem with it is X."

Even if your attempt to persuade them to support the cause fails, many people will remember their impression of you even if they forget everything you actually said. If a person mentions to a friend that they met a nice, polite and thoughtful person from the Cannabis Party that day, this can be just as good for achieving party objectives as defeating a prohibitionist in verbal combat.

How not to Win and Still Lose

Some of the situations that a cannabis law reform activist will find themselves in are like koans. The correct answer or response to a question may not actually answer the question at all. If a grieving mother tells a story of a lost child and asks how cannabis law reform would have helped, it might be best to suggest the tragedy not become politicised. If a dignified senior citizen wants to win the argument, it might be best to let him. He will never tell his friends that he was bested in argument by a Cannabis Party candidate but he might tell them that he met one and found them polite and respectful, unlike the other politicians.

It has to be kept in mind that the mentality the cannabis law reform activist is fighting against is probably insane. This means that anyone undecided about whether cannabis should be legal or not is at least occasionally insane. The practical application of this point is that you can beat your opposition in an argument and still lose support if you send out the wrong emotional message. Many voters will vote for a guy who they would like to have a beer with, which is something to be considered if you like to quote studies and figures. On the flipside of that, many voters will not vote for a candidate if they consider that candidate of a lower social class, which is something to be considered if you like to use words not in the Queen's public vocabulary. It is possible that the best image is one of a person who fluked their way to the top, but every culture will have its own idea of a hero.

The Bush Doctrine in Cannabis Law Reform

Sometimes the most decisive way to demolish an opponent in an argument is to counter their arguments before they are made. Cannabis law reform activists snigger when a character in *The Simpsons* screams "Won't somebody think of the children?", because a form of this question is asked many times. Likewise, many a hippie is tired of hearing people singing "Get a Haircut and Get a Real Job."

There are two main ways that prohibitionists will try and destroy the image of a cannabis law reform activist. The first is to paint the activist as a danger to children and young people, and the second is to paint them as a useless bludger.

A good pre-emptive strike, therefore, will establish to the audience that the activist is a responsible and hard-working person. The ideal would be to lead with a story about how they were on a morning run and saw a twelve-year old push money through the wall of a gang house and get cannabis in return. Having established that the activist is responsible and hard-working, all that remains is to convince the audience that cannabis prohibition does not work.

Another application of the Bush Doctrine is to promote a "with us or against us" mentality that abhors all subtlety and shades of grey in the cannabis issue. An example of this is to accuse everyone who does not vote for a cannabis law reform party to be happy to see people go to prison for cannabis offences. Doing this is really playing with fire and, as such, care needs to be taken that it is the correct move.

How to Explain the Status Quo

Usually, the first question that neutrals will put to cannabis law reform activists is: "If cannabis is as harmless as you say it is, why is it illegal?" This is a difficult question to answer because it could be asked for a lot of reasons and the answer to this question involves a number of factors, many of which sound preposterous. The truth is that the power elites might wish to keep cannabis illegal for a wide variety of reasons that themselves have differing motivations. With a view to winning support for cannabis law reform, it is a good idea, at least initially, to give reasons that suggest the least amount of conspiracy.

Probably the most suitable answer is to say that cannabis was made illegal due to an overreaction by conservative forces which saw it as a mentally destructive drug that drove people criminally insane. Cannabis users were supposedly linked to a number of crimes of violence and property and it has taken until now for science to establish that such behaviour is not caused, or even facilitated by, cannabis. Absurdities such as the propaganda film *Reefer Madness* have been responsible for cannabis acquiring the reputation it has.

Another relatively uncontroversial answer is to say that, because cannabis use first made an impression on the cultural consciousness of the West due to its use by ethnic minorities (in particular Mexican farm workers and blacks in the Southern American states) it was associated with them, and existing racial prejudice conspired to ban it in an effort to give police an excuse to victimise non-white people. The belief that supplying cannabis was a tactic used by ethnic minority males to drug white women into a state where they could not resist a sexual attack has been given as an argument for cannabis prohibition.

To move a little further in the direction of conspiracy, it

has been shown that much of the opposition to cannabis initially came in the form of forestry and farming interests who saw cannabis, in particular the hemp form of it, as a threat to their capital investment. Because hemp can produce an incredible array of products from a given land area in a limited time, it had the potential to upset the market in many industries and was made illegal by politicians in collusion with business interests. Evidence supporting this theory includes the fact that hemp is not psychoactive (at least not if it is smoked) and that farmers were encouraged to grow hemp to aid the Allied war effort in World War II. Related to this is the idea that cannabis prohibition, however it began, is maintained in deference to the alcohol and tobacco lobbies, who stand to lose tremendously if an alternative to their products became legal.

Even more conspiratorial is the suggestion that cannabis, given the breadth of its use, has been made illegal to give police an excuse to unjustifiably search, detain and seize the assets of anyone they do not like, under the pretext that the arresting officer smelt cannabis. Related to this is the idea that cannabis is illegal so that government intelligence agencies can sell it in order to build up a "black budget" which can then be used to fund illegal actions away from the oversight of any auditor.

Perhaps the ultimate conspiracy theory is that cannabis is illegal because it strips away the psychological conditioning that all citizens are exposed to through the education system and through commercial advertising. This view maintains that much of government action is taken to brainwash people into being highly productive, consumerist wage slaves, and that smoking cannabis enables a person to see through the lies and stand up for themselves. Essentially this view suggests that cannabis is illegal because its use makes people harder to control.

There is probably some truth behind all of these explanations, and it requires a thorough reading of Jack Herer's *The Emperor Wears No Clothes* to get an adequate grasp on them. The important thing for the activist is to exercise their discretion as to which one of them best suits their efforts, given the person they are talking to. Any neutral person will likely have certain prejudices about cannabis users that must be defeated, and if an activist mentions the more extreme conspiracy theories - even if they are absolutely correct - they might appear to confirm these prejudices.

Countering Disinformation

What makes arguing for cannabis law reform difficult is that cannabis is a subject that everyone knows a lot about, but most of what they know is wrong. Because of the taboo nature of drugs, there is a vacuum of information that inevitably gets filled by myth and prejudice. Because the cannabis prohibition machine is the classic example of a government policy that has failed to achieve its stated objectives but which continues nonetheless, and which at every stage must justify its continuation, the amount of bullshit it spews out must be countered before any progress can be made.

The single biggest problem that cannabis law reform activists face when discussing cannabis prohibition with members of the public is that people hate the idea that

135

someone has deceived them, and will become angry if this suggestion is made. Many, if not most, people genuinely believe that the government is a servant of the people and therefore everything it says about the harmful effects of cannabis are true: "they couldn't say it if it wasn't true."

Because of this mentality, it is often a poor idea to lead with a suggestion that the government is lying, or that prohibitionists have been suckered (even though this is exactly how it is). The government may or may not be a servant of the people, but in any case, most people are at least aware of a situation in which the government has lied. A cannabis law reform activist can mention Watergate, or the leadup to the Iraq War, and use this to test how naive the person they are speaking to is. If that person concedes that the government is not a dispenser of iron-cast truths, this will form an intellectual beachhead from which an attack on prohibition can be made.

The cannabis law reform activist should at all times speak as if they are in the same boat as the person they are talking to, i.e. "it's us against the system." They should avoid statements such as "the government has lied to you", and should instead use "the government has lied to us." Likewise it's best to emphasise that the government is wasting "our" tax money on prohibition. It can be very effective, if someone makes an argument for prohibition, to begin rebuttal with "yes, that's what I used to think as well, until I discovered that the government was lying to us. Then I found out that the truth is..." It will make the subject of the discussion feel like less of a sucker if the cannabis law reform activist

136

makes clear that they too fell for the same lie when it was first presented.

With this achieved, it becomes possible for the cannabis law reform activist, once they have told someone the truth, to massage that person's self-esteem by suggesting that that person, having been intelligent enough to also see through the lies, is now one of the enlightened ones and is therefore in a better position than the rest of the population. This is true, and if a person can be persuaded that it is the truth they will become far more likely to spread the message of cannabis law reform to others that they know.

When to Push On, and When to Give Up

It is important to take things as far as they will go until resistance is met. Because time and money are limited, maximum advantage has to be sought from every face-to-face encounter.

What this means in practice is that the cannabis law reform activist ought to realise that anyone who agrees with the cannabis law reform argument is a potential voter, and every voter is a potential member or activist.

Although it is easy to believe that, because of the numbers of people affected, cannabis law reform is one of the modern world's foremost human rights issues, many people will never have considered it and some of those will not be receptive to it under any circumstances. The activist must be able to understand where their efforts to gather support are best utilised. Part of this is knowing when they are putting the argument to a person who will never be persuaded.

If a neutral appears to have formed their opinion on cannabis law on an assumption that rests on emotion and not reason, it might not be worth trying to persuade them otherwise. The fact is that many people are simply terrified of cannabis law reform and would expect to see the streets descend into anarchy if it ever came about. If a person appears to believe that the social fabric would disintegrate if cannabis prohibition was lifted, or if they go into a rant about lazy, bludging hippies, or if they use the phrase "devil's weed", it's time to just walk away. Likewise, if a person appears to simply not like you from the instant you initiate contact then don't waste your time. Thank them politely for listening and wish them a good day, without any snide or sarcastic remark. You can't win 'em all, and you don't have to.

1. ARGUMENTS FOR CANNABIS LAW REFORM

Prohibition Doesn't Work

Essentially, all arguments for cannabis law reform are a form of this argument. Even if an activist cannot conclusively demonstrate that a certain position on the legalisation spectrum is superior (and, to be fair, it is hard to use real-world examples), it can always be claimed that cannabis prohibition has failed to achieve any sensible objective.

The key tactic to use here is to examine the claims that prohibitionists make and to demolish them one after the other. Usually, a person in favour of prohibition will claim that it is intended to help one or more particular groups of people, and because of this the best counterargument is to show that it does not.

Cannabis prohibitionists make a myriad of claims as to the supposed benefits of their policy. Although this attack from a hundred directions has shown itself to be historically effective at swaying the balance of public support, it does provide the activist with considerable ammunition with which to destroy their case. It means that the activist can attack where the prohibitionists are weakest. Despite this, it is advisable for the activist to go for full spectrum dominance of the cannabis issue. The truth is that there isn't a single argument that can be made for cannabis prohibition that cannot be countered to some degree.

It is important to note here that a majority of the arguments put forward in favour of cannabis prohibition will, paradoxically, point to harms only caused by cannabis use under a system of prohibition.

The Market Needs to be Regulated

Cannabis prohibitionists spin an image of the cannabis industry being kept in check by the benevolent and omnipresent eye of law enforcement. The truth is that the cannabis industry is closer to anarchy than most other industries of its size (some arguments below will expand on this point). There is no quality control, there is no tax revenue, and there is no way of knowing what the actual effects of cannabis use are.

Once the public becomes aware of the level of chaos within the cannabis industry, few of them will disagree that the market needs to be regulated. Should a cannabis law reform activist decide that the words "legalise" or "decriminalise" carry too much stigma, they can use the word "regulate."

People are naturally afraid of chaos and for this reason the word "regulate" will appeal strongly to them. The converse is also true. Sometimes a problem can be blamed on cannabis prohibition, but other times it is better to blame it on an "unregulated cannabis market." Using phrases like this will also legitimise the cannabis law reform effort by framing the problem in a mainstream vocabulary.

Calling for a regulated cannabis market also pre-empts one of the prohibitionists' most emotive arguments: that cannabis users are irresponsible and enacting cannabis law reform would be negligence on the part of the government. If the problem is the unregulated cannabis market, then the government has the responsibility to introduce regulation.

This point is actually so good that it can be used to recover from almost any position, and will work on almost anyone no matter how closed-minded. No matter how extreme the social effects cannabis is accused of having, a case can be made for regulation being a better approach.

Freedom

Probably the biggest of all the arguments to self interest in favour of cannabis law reform is that of individual freedom. Ultimately, any discussion about where the actions of a state infringe on the rights of the individual is about this. A person does not have to be a libertarian to agree that an individual should be the ultimate arbiter of what chemicals go into their body.

Using this argument requires that a person can be persuaded that they have the right to use cannabis. Because establishing this is complicated and involves a number of assumptions, it is often better to argue that the government does not have the right to prevent individuals from using cannabis, and let that person draw the obvious conclusion.

A very large proportion of neutrals will be receptive to the message that the government is far too intrusive and when they are they will often agree that cannabis prohibition is an example of this. This can be a way of broaching the subject of cannabis law reform in a conversation about something else. If someone makes a disparaging comment about the nanny state or socialism there is a good chance that they will agree that cannabis prohibition is none of the government's business.

The difficulty with using freedom as an argument for cannabis law reform is that it is a very vague concept that cannot be quantified. No one can put a dollar value on a given amount of freedom, and some people want it more than others. A prohibitionist might claim that cannabis prohibition saves a certain amount of money each year, but no one can say if the loss of freedom is worth more than the supposed economic gains. In a given situation and for a given person, the dollar value of freedom could be anywhere from zero to infinite.

The advantage with using freedom as an argument is that almost everyone can identify with it. Almost every child has had the experience of being told by a parent that they were not allowed to do something because "I said so." If an adult can recall feeling angry upon hearing this as a child, they might become angry again if a parallel was drawn between that and the government's current attitude towards cannabis.

Because the freedom argument is almost entirely an emotional one, it will be effective if it causes the listener to feel angry at the government. For this reason, the activist ought to use it on people who are already angry, suspicious or dissatisfied with the government. Because it is an emotional argument it is hard to persuade people that they should value freedom more, so if they appear

142

not to it is probably a good idea to try a different tack.

Libertarians, the self-employed, anyone who appears rebellious (bikers, punks etc.), young adults, atheists or any other freethinker will generally find this argument persuasive. Nanny statists, the religious, social democrats, parents of teenagers and the elderly generally will not.

God Put Cannabis Here

Any cannabis law reform activist will quickly learn that one of the strongest forces behind prohibition is organised religion. In almost every society in the world, it is the religious who most aggressively force others to think along certain lines, and who advocate the most vicious penalties for what they see as misbehaviour. Because the religious are aware that smoking cannabis allows people to see through the lies accepted by society, and because the religious are one of the biggest groups of liars, cannabis is a natural enemy to them.

Despite this unfortunate reality, the holy book of the Christians states that cannabis prohibition goes against the will of God. Genesis 1:29 reads: "And God said, Behold, I have given you every herb bearing seed, which is upon the face of all the earth, and every tree, in which is the fruit of a tree yielding seed; to you it shall be for meat." Given that Christian belief is based on the Bible, it is hard for any Christian to argue for cannabis prohibition and to also stay consistent with scripture.

However, the ability of Christians to believe two contradictory things simultaneously is legendary, and for this reason many will reject arguments for cannabis law reform even though such arguments are supported by the Bible. If an activist finds themselves in this situation it might be best to withdraw and fight somewhere else.

Cannabis is a Religious and Spiritual Sacrament

This argument will appear blasphemous to the more aggressive and established religious traditions in the Western world. It is clear, however, that a number of other religious traditions derive considerable value from cannabis use.

For a Western audience the most obvious example of this is Rastafarianism, who consider cannabis to be the "Tree of Life" mentioned in the Bible. Many of the religions of India also have a place for the effects of the cannabis plant.

Even people who are not steeped in the mindset of a particular religion have found a spiritual value in using cannabis. Many feel that the cannabis high awakens a part of the mind that is not materialistic, and as a consequence they come to understand the interrelatedness of all things, which leads to a greater connection to the Earth and the things in it. Perhaps this reveals a clue as to why cannabis is illegal in the first place, but nonetheless it is considered a basic human right in Western society that people have freedom of religion, and therefore there should be no legal restrictions on how a person's religious sentiments are discovered and expressed.

It's hard to know who would be persuaded by this

argument. Followers of most traditional religious practices will generally resist the idea that truth can be found through smoking cannabis, for the obvious reason that doing so will reveal their own truth as lies. This argument might carry the most weight amongst those of a New Age persuasion.

Cannabis is an Established Crop I

Many people who are not part of the cannabis culture do not understand how big the cannabis industry is, even in places where it is illegal. The image in the popular consciousness seems to be of shady gang members who grow a few plants in a mountain park somewhere and, through a convoluted procedure designed to avoid the police, sell it to the occasional trembling, wretched drug addict. The truth is, of course, that cannabis is churned out by the pound and only a very small percentage of the market ever comes to the attention of law enforcement.

In fact, the cannabis industry is already so large that cannabis is the number one cash crop in over a dozen states of the USA and in many other places. Considering the volumes of other foodstuffs produced by these places, this means that there are massive amounts of cannabis already on the black market.

This argument essentially states that the cannabis industry is so large that it cannot be exterminated, and because of this it deserves its place at the table as a legitimate major industry. It is hard to estimate what the size of the industry would be in a system without prohibition, because there are not many real world examples to point to. It is fair to assume that the hemp industry alone has the potential to rival the largest of the others, to say nothing of the use of the psychoactive components of cannabis in medicines and recreation.

This argument may be of little use in garnering votes, but it will speak to the politicians and the business interests who are both on the lookout for new economic potential and have far more influence than the average cannabis law reform voter.

Cannabis is an Established Crop II

This is a variation of the "you'll never get rid of it anyway" argument described above. The difference is that this argument refers to the place of cannabis in the national culture, not in its economy.

Although the figures change with every new survey (and the cannabis law reform activist must always keep up to date), it cannot be denied that there are multitudes of people smoking cannabis in our societies. It is so established that Hollywood films are made in which the entire plot revolves around cannabis, and few are the adults who would not recognise the sight or smell of the cannabis plant.

Making this argument is the same as saying that the War on Drugs has been lost, or at least is going so badly that no victory is possible. This is true, but this point must always be followed with an argument that cannabis law reform is better, otherwise its effect is wasted.

This argument comes with a booster. Cannabis is already entrenched in the national consciousness, and it is even more so with the younger generation. Because they will themselves become older, and the next generation will likely be even more cannabis friendly, the tide of history is clearly in favour of cannabis law reform.

This argument will work best on people who are realistic and pragmatic. The main advantage of it is that it will appeal to people who are not cannabis users themselves.

Effectiveness of the Police

Cannabis prohibition ties up a large amount of police time and resources that could be better spent fighting serious crime. The beauty of this argument is that it can be used in reference to any situation in which the police have failed to respond to a call in time, or where a police investigation has failed due to lack of resources. If the activist has information about how many police hours are spent on a yearly basis enforcing prohibition, these can be given.

A consequence of cannabis prohibition is that cannabis users come to see the police as the enemy, and might not call them if they observe a crime being committed, for fear that any encounter with the police will lead to their own arrest. They are also far less likely to respond to a call for assistance that a police officer might make. If the police make a public request for information, anyone in possession of cannabis is much less likely to respond, even if they have information crucial to the investigation.

This argument could work on anyone, because most people have not considered the view of the police from the perspective of a cannabis user. Conservatives are usually happy to hear of any suggestion that increases the effectiveness of and respect for the police, and other people are likewise generally supportive of anything that makes it more difficult for actual criminals to get away with what they have done.

Effectiveness of the Prisons

Tied in very closely with the previous argument, cannabis prohibition costs every country considerable resources that are spent incarcerating cannabis offenders. Because prison sentences for cannabis offences are generally given to people who are not violent, considerable psychological damage is done by putting them in prison with those that are, which has related social costs. In many countries there is often a shortage of space in prisons. Because of this it can be suggested that repealing prohibition will allow the corrections system to avoid the necessity of releasing other prisoners early to make space for those convicted of cannabis offences

Related to the effectiveness of the prisons is that cannabis law reform would prevent cannabis users from being locked up in a place where they essentially are granted an education in how to commit crime. A person who is sent to prison for a cannabis offence may or may not be a criminal when they go in, but the chances are very high that they will be a criminal by the time they get out. While inside, not only will they develop a hatred for the justice system and those who work to enable it, but there is also a high chance that they will get recruited into a criminal gang, which makes it more likely that

that person will turn to serious crime when they get out.

This argument will appeal to almost anyone, because both conservatives and social democrats will think less of cannabis prohibition if it can be argued that it makes people into criminals.

The Effect on Respect for the Law and for the Police

Many people are aware of the stupidity of cannabis prohibition. Unfortunately, because it is a law, any police officer who has sworn to uphold the law must act to enforce it. This has some sociological side-effects that do not help either citizens or the police. Anyone who does not believe that cannabis is a crime will experience three effects.

The first is a loss of respect for the police that enforce prohibition. To a cannabis user there is little difference between a police officer entering a home to arrest someone for possession of cannabis or for possession of a pack of cigarettes. Naturally this leads to outrage and eventually hatred towards law enforcement officers. In many other regards, the police are the citizen's first or second line of defence against criminal action, so for a person to lose faith in this is a tragedy. A consequence of this loss of respect is that upstanding citizens who would make excellent police officers might feel themselves unsuited for the profession because they cannot morally justify to themselves the need to arrest and imprison people who are only criminals because of a whim of the law. It should be noted here that police officers in the Netherlands do not have this problem and this is reflected in the much higher esteem in which they are

149

held by the citizenry, especially the young.

The second is a loss of respect for the law itself. If all it takes for a police officer to enter someone's home and physically restrain them is for permission to be written in a law book, then a natural consequence is for people to question the validity of the law. If one law can be so blatantly unjust, why not others? Indeed, why not the legal system itself? Once a person has made the decision to violate laws relating to cannabis prohibition they have less reason to follow the others, because the justification for them will also fall under suspicion.

The third is a loss of respect for the entire political system. There are few words dirtier than "criminal", because to commit crime is to behave so barbarically that one must be punished in order to maintain civil peace. In many Western countries this means that a majority of the population are criminals. Few of them, however, consider themselves criminals, because the vast majority are good people just trying to get through life.

This argument is best used on people of a conservative persuasion, because conservatives generally have more respect for the police and will be more unhappy to learn that others do not.

The Punishment Does Not Fit the Crime

A basic principle of any system of justice is that the severity of the punishment must be in proportion to the harm caused by the offending. Common assault is not punished as hard as doing grievous bodily harm to someone, which in turn is not punished as hard as murder. Without this principle in place, the citizenry lose faith in the justice system to deliver justice.

There is perhaps no other crime in which the punishment is more disproportionately severe than the range of cannabis offences (there cannot be if the net harm is nil), for the simple reason that cannabis is a crime without a victim. If a cannabis law reform activist monitors the newspapers in their area or country they will soon discover a case in which a crime of sex or violence resulted in a lesser punishment than was handed down in another case where only cannabis was involved. This is an excellent time to write a letter to the local paper pointing out the discrepancy. Cases are common in which a careless, dangerous or drunk driver kills a cyclist or a pedestrian and are given lighter sentences than the man in the previous court session was for growing a medicine.

A cannabis law reform activist in New Zealand, at being sentenced for growing a cannabis plant, told the judge "I would like to apply for restorative justice. I would like to apologise to the victim of my crime." The courtroom tittered, but this simple statement laid bare the absurdity of the prohibition system. His punishment did not fit the crime; it could never have done because no crime had been committed.

This argument is best used on people who are already supporters of cannabis law reform, because the less of a crime someone considers cannabis use to be the more outrageous any penalty for it will appear. This will help to fire them up and make them more willing to take future action on behalf of cannabis law reform.

The Effect of Criminal Records is Disproportionate

This is related to the previous point, but deals not with the severity of a sentence but with the effects of a criminal conviction, even one that did not result in imprisonment. In most jurisdictions, a criminal conviction for a cannabis offence will stay on that individual's criminal record for the rest of their life. If they are arrested, tried and convicted of possession of cannabis at age 25, they will be forced to declare this, if asked, at age 55. This is despite the fact that many current politicians have admitted prior cannabis use, which, presumably, would have affected their political careers should it have resulted in a conviction.

There are a number of consequences to having a criminal record. A number of employers will not hire anyone with a criminal record no matter what that crime is. On top of this, many countries will not allow entry to anyone with a criminal record, which damages the potential of anyone self-employed. For young people, who make up the bulk of people charged with cannabis offences, a criminal conviction can result in massive loss of earning potential and productivity over the remainder of their life.

There is probably no mileage to be gained from further evidence that politicians are hypocrites, however there are many people who can be persuaded that a criminal conviction is an excessive punishment for possessing cannabis. The advantage of this argument is that it works on not only cannabis users, but anyone concerned with the welfare of a relation who is. The elderly (who vote in great numbers), if they have a grandchild who might be a cannabis user, can find a lot to agree with in this argument.

It is an Alternative to Booze

The basis of this argument is that, because people will take drugs in order to have a good time, it's best if they are able to take drugs that do less damage than others. Because alcohol has been shown to result in a considerable amount of violent crime, some of this could be avoided if people had access to cannabis instead. There are so many news reports of violent crime in which the police are quoted as saying "alcohol may have been involved" that it has become a cliché

The argument doesn't end at violent crime either; there are many work days lost because people are recovering from hangovers, and the physical effects of alcohol over time can be deadly due to causes such as liver and kidney disease (alcohol is a poison; cannabis is a medicine).

To some people this will be a very poor argument. As long as people see cannabis as a "hard drug" (a category that, for some reason, never includes alcohol) they will be appalled to hear an argument that people should be smoking it instead of drinking. In many cases, their line of reasoning will be "why should the government allow more dangerous substances instead of fewer?" If a person appears to think like this, it's probably best to write them off as a fascist and fight elsewhere.

153

Other Legal Drugs Have an Acceptable Level of Harm Which is Higher than that of Cannabis

The strength of this argument is in that it points out that our current drug laws are inconsistent. The main thrust of the prohibitionist argument is that cannabis is so dangerous that it must be made illegal as a disincentive, the logic being that the harms it causes are thereby reduced because of fewer people smoking it from fear of legal consequences.

Cannabis law reform activists can here point out that the harms done by alcohol and tobacco, not to mention pharmaceuticals, are considerably greater than those done by cannabis, and yet these harms are not considered enough to make those drugs illegal. It is estimated that tobacco alone kills over 400,000 Americans per year, and while it is harder to accurately measure the damage caused by alcohol it is certainly higher than that caused by cannabis.

Given that, in cases where cannabis prohibition has been relaxed, usage of cannabis has either stayed around the same or has gone down, it can be asked where the sense is in keeping cannabis illegal, at great cost, when society has already proven itself to be stable enough to absorb the damage done by other drugs?

An Ethnic Rights Perspective I

Many of the territories in which cannabis is illegal were conquered relatively recently by invaders from outside that territory. In most of these cases, the populations that previously dominated that territory still exist, and many of them do not accept the laws of the invaders.

Although the ethnic rights argument will appeal to few outside of the ethnicity in question, the basic thrust of this argument is that cannabis was not illegal according to the legal codes of many conquered peoples, and therefore anyone who follows these codes are not bound to observe cannabis prohibition.

In practice, it might be better to use this argument in a court of law than when agitating for cannabis law reform. Most native peoples of the New World can make an argument for the illegitimacy of the court, and in the likely event this fails can then go on to argue that the values of the culture in which they were raised and in which they live accepts cannabis use, the implication being that the court should respect this culture.

An argument that might have more traction amongst the majority population relates to the potential of the establishment to use cannabis prohibition as a weapon against minority populations. Although police officers generally do not have the right of discretion with regards to who they arrest and who they do not, in practice it is well known that it is common for police to let a white person off a cannabis charge when they would not do the same for a black person or a native. This explains why blacks and others make up a far higher proportion of cannabis arrests than their activity in cannabis culture would suggest. On top is this it is broadly known that white people get more lenient sentences than others when it comes to cannabis offences that do make it to court, partially because of fewer prior convictions and aggravating circumstances, but also because of institutional racism within the justice system.

For these reasons it can be argued that cannabis law reform would help enforce a state of racial equality before the law. This argument will appeal to ethnic minorities and social democrats more than anyone else. It also serves a probe argument: if an activist mentions this argument to a white person who dismisses it out of hand, implying through word or action that the fate of the underclass is of little importance to them, that person is very likely to give consideration to arguments about freedom and the economic cost of prohibition.

An Ethnic Rights Perspective II

This applies more to the native peoples of the New World than to anywhere else, although it could appeal to many ethnic groups across the world.

When the colonial empires of Europe attacked the peoples of the rest of the world, one of the first things they did was supply the natives with alcohol. It was known by the aggressors that alcohol would have a disintegrating effect on the cultures and peoples who were not used to it, and the natives who became addicted to it found themselves unable to resist further encroachment upon their territories.

The Europeans were, of course, used to alcohol: they had had access to it for thousands of years and the individuals amongst them who were most vulnerable to the worst effects of it had long since died out, leaving a population that was comparably resistant. It is known that people of European ancestry have enzymes within their bodies that make them less likely to succumb to alcoholism.

The natives of the New World have not had thousands of years to adapt to ingestion of alcohol, and a quick look at rates of alcoholism amongst the different ethnic groups of the New World shows this. Because most countries in the New World are dominated by white politicians, they are the ones who have decided that alcohol shall be legal and cannabis not, and this does not produce a level playing field for the individuals who can only access what is legal. Legalising cannabis would effectively be a truce in the chemical war that white people are conducting against the populations they have subjugated.

The difficulty with using this argument is that many people believe that the higher rates of alcoholism amongst native populations are because of a mental weakness or moral failing, and that these peoples therefore deserve what they get. Likewise, many leaders of native populations don't consider cannabis to be any better than alcohol, at least in part because they have also bought into the establishment propaganda. Still, it can be used when talking to members of native populations who are aware that white politicians are not to be trusted, which is all of them.

Cannabis Suits Some People Better than Alcohol Does

Anyone who has worked in a bar, or who has been to several parties amongst the same group of friends, will have become aware that a certain percentage of individuals cannot handle their liquor. Those who watch them get drunk are familiar with the feeling of dread that arises when they realise something stupid is about to be done. Some call it the 90/10 rule: 90 percent of drinkers are fine, but that last 10 percent is responsible for 90 percent of the drunken crimes.

Some of the people in that 10 percent are simply idiots who will fly off the handle for any reason, drunk, stoned or sober, but many of them are people who would be better off smoking cannabis. The drunks who do the most damage are the bad-tempered, aggressive ones, and for them to have access to a drug that calmed them down and made them more passive would be a benefit to everyone. On top of this, there is a large number of people who would be fine on either alcohol or cannabis but, when given the choice, would prefer cannabis because it agrees with them more.

This argument works best on anyone who has been the victim of alcohol-related violence, whether directly or indirectly. Since there are very large numbers of such victims this argument has a lot of mileage.

A Youth Perspective

When looking at survey results on attitudes to cannabis, it becomes clear that there is a considerable generational divide. The generation of people who are now retired were brought up on *Reefer Madness* and still have the tendency to believe what they're told by the government. If they are white, chances are good that none of their friends were cannabis users when they were young, and that they have never tried cannabis themselves.

The generation of people who have recently come of voting age, their older siblings, and, to a lesser extent, their parents, tend to have different opinions. Older people stayed away from cannabis partly because their government told them it was bad, and partly because they were more influenced by a more Puritan mentality. The younger generation is increasingly turning away from alcohol and towards cannabis because, as time passes, it is becoming clearer that cannabis is more fun. For this reason, relatively fewer young people are supporters of cannabis prohibition.

It can, and should, be argued, that cannabis is now an accepted part of youth culture, and that its criminalisation is generational warfare committed by the old people who make up the vast majority of politicians. A look at over 2,000 years of Western history shows that, at any point in time, the elders of society were concerned about the moral degeneration of the young whereas the young were concerned with the restrictions placed on their behaviour by the old. For this reason, a vote for cannabis law reform can be sold as a vote against unreasonable restrictions being placed on the young by the old.

When making a cannabis law reform argument from a young person's perspective to someone who is middle-aged or older, the activist might well discover that the person they are talking to harbours concerns about the out of control nature of youth and the crimes of violence and property that they are believed to be committing in record numbers. The activist can take the approach of agreeing with them that things are out of hand, and then point out that almost all of the stupid things that young people do are done when they are drunk. If the subject of the conversation does not themselves suggest the obvious solution, the activist can: many of these crimes, especially not the violent ones, would not have occurred if the perpetrator had gone down to a cannabis café instead of a bottle store and got high instead of drunk.

Old people are not likely to put much stock in the feelings of the youth when they go to vote. However, the youth are their own worst enemy because they do not vote at anywhere near the same levels as the old. If a cannabis law reform activist is speaking to a group of young people, chances are good that they will already agree with the legalisation message, and what they can help do to repeal prohibition, so all the emphasis should go on persuading them that it is important to actually turn up on election day and cast their vote, as well as tell every friend they have that this is what they plan to do.

A Baby Boomer Perspective

The Baby Boomers are seen by some as the personification of all that is good and all that is bad in Western society. Born in the decades following the Second World War, many of them came to age in the Swinging Sixties, where, for a brief but indelible number of years, they formed a movement of creative, drug and sexual freedom that attacked the American establishment from within more successfully than the Third Reich and the Empire of Japan could do from without.

Hunter S. Thompson's character in *Fear and Loathing in Las Vegas*, set in 1971, noted a point where "with the right kind of eyes you can almost *see* the high-water

160

mark – that place where the wave finally broke and rolled back." The practical consequence of this watershed was that the hippie movement largely abandoned the trappings of the culture they had built and got corporate jobs, homes in the suburbs, and families to fill them.

Now the first of the baby boomers have recently entered retirement. The entire cohort will follow in the next few decades, in numbers the Western pension system has never before seen. The perceptions of Generations X and Y is that the Boomers are the single greediest and self-obsessed generation that ever lived; a moral antithesis to the "Greatest Generation" who pulled America out of the Great Depression and whose blood and courage won the Second World War.

All this may or not be believed by the Boomers themselves or by the cannabis law reform activists trying to turn them on to our message. However, it is clear that arguments put to Baby Boomers must, first and last, explain how cannabis law reform will help them in their current situation.

As they age, they will come to demand more and more medicine and health care, and therefore a working knowledge of the benefits of medical marijuana will be crucial to winning support from this large and heavily voting cohort. They will also be especially interested to hear about how the nation can save money that could be used for the hole in pension liabilities, or which could even mitigate the expected increase in the retirement age.

The Economic Future Will be Based on Innovation and Creativity

It has long been known that cannabis is the favourite drug of creative people. It first became popular in the United States partially due to the fact that the jazz musicians of the Deep South liked to smoke it before gigs, finding that it aided their ability to improvise. As the comedian Bill Hicks pointed out, many of the musicians that have produced the music that people have loved since the sixties composed their work while high on cannabis.

Because the focus of economic advancement is moving away from manufacturing and monotonous repetition of facts learned by rote, and towards innovative practices, there is an economic incentive to legalise a drug that would facilitate innovation. In much the same way as modern industrial office culture is built around caffeine, the future might be built around cannabis. Cannabis makes it easier for people to look at things from new perspectives, and because of this people can see where improvements can be made on the old way of doing things.

This argument will appeal most strongly to the generation of young people who have discovered that the existing economic order expects them to slot in at the bottom of the hierarchy and to slowly work their way up over time, as well as to current business owners who intend to employ "knowledge workers" or creative types.

Prohibition Helps the Gangs and Other Criminals

Another problem with cannabis prohibition is that, because the demand for it is there, a market for it will always exist. Making cannabis illegal has done little or nothing to stop the prevalence of its use, and has merely driven its trade underground. There are several problems with having cannabis on the black market.

The first is the loss of tax revenue. For obvious reasons, sales of cannabis on the black market do not attract sales or income taxes for the central government. Given the size of the cannabis trade, this represents a considerable loss of revenue, and, given the ease with which the cannabis trade could be regulated, this income could easily be gathered.

The second is that it strengthens the gangs and other criminal organisations who always meet existing demand for goods and services that are illegal. Because they can easily sell cannabis to a large number of people, the gangs derive considerable income from cannabis prohibition. This can then be used to expand the gang's activity into financing the importation of other drugs, sex slaves or weapons and could also be used to pay off police or politicians.

The third is that making cannabis illegal is effectively the same as making the trade unregulated. This means that there are no restrictions on who cannabis can be sold to, nor to the purity or quality of the good. Criminal gangs could not care less if they sold cannabis to someone too young to deal with the psychological consequences of smoking it, and neither are they averse to lacing it with fly spray if they believe that this will make it look more appealing.

The fourth is that, because the production and sale of cannabis requires considerable physical resources, it is not especially economical, which means that there is an incentive for gangs to peddle harder, more profitable drugs to customers who initially only wanted cannabis. There are countless examples of people who wanted to buy cannabis being forced to approach a gang, whereupon they are offered methamphetamine or heroin and thereby become addicted to those.

Anyone who believes that cannabis should be illegal is effectively supporting these four things, and should be told in no uncertain terms that this is the effect of prohibition. The anti-gang argument appeals to a very broad section of the voting public and can be used on almost anyone (except, obviously, gang members).

Prohibition Creates and Protects Drug Cartels

This argument is similar to the one above it, and many of the points above are relevant here, but a drug cartel is an entirely higher level of operation to a street gang, and its operations involve far greater organisation, far more ruthless behaviour and far more money.

Enforcement of prohibition ruins the lives of huge numbers of people, but the drug cartels themselves continue to operate despite this. This is because the people at the top of them do not get arrested, and the members of the cartels who do are easily replaced. In cases where cannabis is confiscated, the cartels do lose

164

some money, but this is factored into their equations as a cost of doing business.

When a drug cartel gets big enough it can use some of the profits it generates to bribe people in law enforcement to turn a blind eye to the activity of the cartel. Given the size of the cannabis market it is not surprising that this happens, and this is precisely what happened under alcohol prohibition.

Because of these reasons, cannabis prohibition, whatever its intention, has the effect of keeping cartels in business by striking at anyone else who could be a competitor. It increases the price and helps destroy the competitors who fight for the turf on which to sell their product. Cannabis law reform would do to these cartels what alcohol law reform did to Al Capone and his gangsters.

A lot of people will see the merit of the argument, especially if they have been victimised at the hands of the drug cartels.

Cannabis Prohibition Allows Terrorists to Fund Themselves

Because terrorist groups are, by definition, illegal, they have no way of making an income other than by breaking the law. A consequence of this is that they can, and will, make money through the black market. The larger the black market is, the more possibility there is for criminal groups to generate income and to expand and thrive.

To make an argument on this point, a cannabis law

reform activist will first have to establish in the minds of their listeners that cannabis prohibition does not make cannabis disappear, but merely shifts it to the black market.

Cannabis law reform is an attack on the black market, because it regulates the production and sale of cannabis under the law. Any organisation that depends on cannabis prohibition in order to exist will consequently wither and die.

This argument will work on anyone who does not like terrorist groups, which is almost everyone. It is essentially the same argument as the one against criminal gangs.

Cannabis is a Medicine

Unfortunately, this is an argument that tends to bring derisive laughter from the prohibitionists. Mocking cries of "you just want an excuse to get high" is the typical response, which is cruel for those millions who have discovered that cannabis is a far more effective medicine, with considerably fewer side-effects, than those pushed by the pharmaceutical industry. Part of this response is a result of the suspicion that advocating medicinal marijuana is a trojan horse for the full legalisation of cannabis for all citizens. This suspicion might be correct, but it does not weaken the argument for cannabis as a medicine.

The medicinal properties of cannabis have been known for over 3,500 years. Papyrus from ancient Egypt describes medicinal cannabis and its uses, as does a

Chinese medical textbook dating from 100 B.C. Few Westerners know that cannabis was the primary medicinal source of pain relief in the 19th century and up until the invention of aspirin, with over 2,000 cannabis-based products manufactured by several hundred manufacturers. Cynics might point out here that the advent of a patented medicine that provided a means for drug companies to make a profit where none existed before narrowly preceded cannabis prohibition.

The growth of medical marijuana dispensaries in the USA shows that there is a large number of people who find cannabis an effective medicine for their ailments, in particular pain relief and appetite promotion. For people who are suffering from cancer or from the side-effects of treatments for cancer, both of these benefits have a considerable influence on their quality of life. The other uses of medicinal cannabis are too numerous to go into here, but even the most rudimentary research will reveal dozens of them.

Many people are surprised to learn than cannabis can be and is used as a medicine, because the image of cannabis that they are presented with is invariably one of young people destroying their lives in the manner depicted by *Reefer Madness*. The argument that cannabis is a medicine is especially strong for elderly citizens, who often find themselves taking medicines that are not especially effective. On top of this, the physical side effects of modern medicines are difficult for people with frail constitutions to deal with.

The argument for medicinal cannabis is a very strong one for cannabis law reform activists: not only would it allow an effective medicine to become available to those who most need it, but those who most need it belong to the demographic that invariably votes.

Cannabis is a Tool for Personal Growth

It is said that variety is the spice of life. The reason for this is that it is necessary to have new experiences in order to have any personal growth; without new experiences people will stagnate. Using cannabis, whether or not one has an enjoyable experience, is something new, and people who do it will learn things about themselves.

If a person smokes cannabis and becomes anxious and paranoid, they might learn that they are a person who needs a certain level of security in order to feel comfortable. If they get high and have a laugh and a good time, they might learn that there is light-hearted fun to be had in the world. If they fall deep into personal rumination they might learn that there are new ways of looking at their problems and that they need never be stuck in a rut. If they become inspired by a new idea or a new pattern of thought they might learn that there are many ways of looking at life and that some of those are better in some situations.

The problem with this argument is that those who buy it are likely to be supporters of cannabis law reform anyway. Those who are supporters of cannabis prohibition have little to gain from allowing other people to grow. For these reasons, this argument is probably best used to inspire those who are already supporters of cannabis law reform to become more active.

168

Quality Control

One point that needs to be continually made is that "banning" cannabis does not mean that the drug no longer exists. It simply means that its production, supply and sale falls under the control of the black market, i.e. criminals who operate with no oversight.

Although it is rarely true that criminal suppliers of cannabis lace the drug with other drugs (it is not economical to do so, amongst other reasons), there is little stopping them from lacing it with fly spray if they believe that this will make the product look more appealing to people who judge cannabis based on its stickiness and shine. This would not occur if cannabis was legalised, because companies who supplied it would not get away with it and people who grew cannabis in their own homes would not do it.

A related point is that, with supply controlled by the black market, there is no reliable way to produce cannabis with a given level of THC. If a person is looking for a mild high to just relax, they could well end up with hydroponic cannabis that is far stronger than what they need. Imagine if the alcohol industry sold bottles of their product in which the alcohol content was anywhere between 2% and 40%, and the customer had no way of knowing what it was until they sampled it. This is much like cannabis on the black market.

This argument has little impact on prohibitionists, because they will retort that "people shouldn't be smoking it anyway so they deserve what they get." To use this argument effectively, a cannabis law reform activist must first persuade the listener that a change in the law is necessary for reasons of harm minimisation, and then use this point to explain how legalisation would reduce harm.

It is a Colossal Waste of Money

This is perhaps the strongest argument for cannabis law reform, not because it is moral but precisely because it is not. Because few people vote based on what they consider to be best for society but upon what is best for themselves, cannabis law reform will appear to be a low priority if they do not smoke it. The cannabis law reform activist's trump card is to inform them of how much money is spent on the Drug War, how much of it is wasted, and how much it costs every individual taxpayer.

Because the figures vary from country to country, the cost of prohibition must be calculated by activists based on their country's figures. This is not difficult, and is done in three steps. Firstly, it must be learned how many people are in prison for cannabis offences and how much it costs to keep each one of them in prison for a year. Multiplying these figures together gives the total expenditure for the corrections system in fighting the Drug War. Secondly, it is necessary to determine the number of hours spent every year in policing cannabis prohibition, and then the average cost in employing a police officer for one hour. Again these figures must be multiplied to give the total expenditure for the police force in fighting the Drug War. Thirdly, it must be determined how many court hours are devoted to prosecuting people for cannabis crimes per year, and the average cost in keeping a court in session for one hour. Multiplying these two figures gives the total expenditure for the court system in fighting the Drug War. Adding together the cost of prisons, police and the courts gives a figure for how much the criminal justice system must spend every year in its efforts to enforce cannabis prohibition.

Most people will be stunned by the final figure. Even in a tiny country such as New Zealand (pop. 4.5 million) this figure is close to half a billion dollars per year, all of it paid for by the taxpayer. It seems, therefore, that every citizen pays a hundred dollars a year to enforce cannabis prohibition alone. For a massive country such as the USA the figure might be around 30 billion dollars.

Furthermore, this figure does not even represent the full cost to a society of cannabis prohibition. Money spent on propaganda can be added to this, as can the lost earning potential of people who are in prison. So can the opportunity cost of economic practices that are made impossible by prohibition.

By far the largest, and most obvious, opportunity cost is lost taxation money. Under a system of prohibition, all of the money generated by the sale of cannabis goes straight into the hands of the criminal gangs that supply it. In California, medical marijuana dispensaries pay $100,000,000 in taxes to the federal government every year, and extrapolating this to the entire USA on a per capita basis suggests that close to a billion dollars would be paid, per year, in taxes from medical marijuana dispensaries alone. It is hard to estimate what the size of the national cannabis market is, for the obvious reason that it is hard to collect figures on black market activity, but it stands to reason that sales taxes and perhaps even vice taxes (following the alcohol and tobacco models) would generate several times this figure.

The Effect on Social Cohesion

This argument is that cannabis prohibition has a detrimental effect on social solidarity, which is a necessary component of any nation or community. Without solidarity, people do not care about the sufferings of others in their neighbourhood or country, and will do nothing to help should an opportunity arise. To understand the deleterious effect of cannabis prohibition on social cohesion, it is necessary to perform a thought experiment that puts a person in the place of a cannabis user.

If you are walking the streets with cannabis in your pocket, you can be arrested and thrown in jail. Let's say you are on a walk, and you see a gang of thieves breaking into a shop. Do you call the police when you know that you yourself will be arrested when they come and ask you to make a statement?

If, at home, you have just charfed back a cone and you look out your window and see that your neighbour's house is on fire, what do you do? Probably you ring them up or go next door to scream across the fence and, should there be no response, you call the fire department, but you don't want to be there when the police arrive – they will want a statement, so they will smell cannabis on you and arrest you.

If someone gets drunk and punches someone in the face in an unprovoked attack, and the aggressor knows that you possess a considerable amount of cannabis at home, and tells you that if you testify against him he will dob you in, what do you do?

There are dozens of examples like this, showing the effect that cannabis prohibition has on the effectiveness of the justice system. Someone possessing cannabis will do almost anything they can to avoid contact with the police, even if that contact would be necessary to ensure that an evil deed gets punished as it should. Because as many as one in every ten people are in possession of cannabis at any given time, this adds up to a lot of people who are forced to act in an asocial manner for fear of consequences to themselves.

Of course, these are only the obvious examples. Cannabis prohibition also has a subtle effect on social cohesion: cannabis users come to hate the people who they know are prohibitionists, for the simple reason that those people are supporting a system that would see the cannabis user locked in a cage and his possessions stolen. When a person knows that his fellow man could lift cannabis prohibition by a simple act of voting, and that man elects not to do so, it is natural and inevitable that the cannabis user come to hate him.

The War on Drugs is a War by Governments on Their Own People

The term "War on Drugs" is a deception, because in cases where a person is arrested in possession of a drug it is that person who suffers the punishment, not the drug. This might sound trivial, but it is crucial. It reflects the fact that governments of countries where cannabis prohibition exists have claimed the right to conduct warfare against their own citizens if those citizens do not behave in a way the government likes.

It can be argued that this is always the case; governments will respond to a failure to pay taxes with at least as much aggression as they enforce cannabis prohibition. This, however, is to miss the point. For a government to claim legitimacy for what it does, it must not conduct warfare against those it claims to represent.

The unappreciated side of the War on Drugs is that, because people have come to understand that it is based on lies, they have begun to make generalisations about other areas of government propagandising. When the government buys television ads that inform people of the dangers of smoking cigarettes, some people no longer trust them because of the lies about cannabis. This is a tragedy because truthful information about tobacco use has the potential to save millions of lives and prevent considerable health problems.

This argument will generally only work on people left of centre, because they tend to believe in the importance of having a big government and will therefore understand that the size of the government is a function of what the people allow, and that what they allow is a function of the trust they have in it.

Cannabis Prohibition Corrupts the Youth

The Western economic and social system is based on a

174

set of obligations that every individual is intended to acknowledge. A child is born, they become educated and then they work. The better educated a person is, the higher the value of their work and the more they are paid. The system, therefore, provides economic and social incentives for individuals to better themselves and to better the situation of their fellows.

Cannabis prohibition corrupts this entire process, because it provides an avenue for people to get rich without having to be educated or to work. If a young person is too lazy, stupid or arrogant to get ahead in a conventional manner they can simply sell cannabis. Any of their peers who have tried to earn a living through increasing the value of their labour and by working hard will see this and feel like suckers. They might decide that crime is an easier way of getting ahead and turn to it. Given that the deck is already heavily stacked against young people, this temptation will at all times be very strong.

This is not to imply that the act of selling cannabis is immoral. Cannabis law reform would ensure that cannabis is sold by small businesses such as cannabis cafés who would be supplied by licensed growers. This system of regulation would ensure that the production and sale of cannabis was taxed appropriately and with sufficient oversight.

The beauty of this argument is that it will work on people of a more conservative persuasion. Conservatives will understand that people have to be correctly incentivised in order to contribute to society, and will understand that cannabis prohibition corrupts this process.

Cannabis Prohibition Destroys Families

One of the largest of the failures in understanding the damage done by cannabis prohibition comes when people fail to understand that individuals who are punished for cannabis offences are part of a network of other people, all of whom are weakened by the destruction wrought upon the offender. Although this damage is done to society as a whole, it is also done to every subunit within society, and the one that takes the most damage is always the family.

If a woman and the children she has borne are dependent on a man for the income they need to buy food and medicine, and if that man gains his income through selling cannabis, arresting him and putting him in prison removes the income that his family depended upon. The effect on his family is extreme. If the woman cannot replace this income, the children will suffer.

Children of families broken up by cannabis prohibition do not suffer only in terms of reduced income. They also miss the opportunity for love and learning that is provided by the parent who is now removed from their environment. It is accepted by all that a father who abandons his children leaves them at a massive disadvantage; it is accepted by few that imprisoning the father for a cannabis offence has precisely the same effect. A father who willingly abandons his children is viewed by many as the lowest kind of scum, but, amazingly, the people who enforce a system whereby that father is taken away are not.

Only the most stony-hearted psychopath could fail to be moved by the sight of a child asking their mother "When is Daddy coming home?" when no satisfactory answer can be given. Yet, in homes throughout any area in which cannabis prohibition is enforced, this phenomenon is commonplace.

In a way, the effect on the children from having a parent incarcerated is worse than the effect from them being abandoned. If a child is abandoned they will grow up to hate their father; if their father is taken away by the police they will grow up to hate society. Many conservatives are outraged when teenagers commit violent crimes, and they scream for heavier punishment, appearing oblivious to the fact that it is precisely the fact that people are punished unnecessarily that makes them violent.

It should be pointed out that the destruction of a family can occur whether it is the father or the mother who is punished for the cannabis offence, but in the vast majority of cases it will be the father.

The argument that cannabis prohibition destroys families is very strong because almost anyone can be persuaded of the logic of it, and almost everyone agrees that, without a strong family unit, the chances of any children produced by one making a positive contribution to society is drastically reduced.

Certain Arguments Must be Used With Caution

Some arguments in favour of cannabis law reform are common but are not persuasive, and others are

177

persuasive to some people but have counterarguments that make the cannabis law reform activist appear foolish and their position ill-considered.

The classic example of this is the argument that "cannabis is natural." This is usually given in reference to the myriad of pharmaceutical drugs that are on offer for all manner of ailments, many of which have undesirable side effects. The argument goes that nature is good, and because cannabis is a part of nature it must also be good. The flaw in this argument is obvious: many things that are natural are definitely not good, such as nightshade.

Another poor argument is to say that, because so many people are using cannabis anyway, it should be legal. The flaw in this argument is that there are plenty of crimes that are committed by large numbers of people, and there is no reason to make any of these activities legal (traffic offences are the example usually given). Having said that, the numbers of people using cannabis suggest that there are comparatively few who see it as a crime, unlike traffic offences.

Another common mistake is to attack alcohol and alcohol users. People who enjoy drinking alcohol are often the same sort of people who would enjoy using cannabis, and they will not support cannabis law reform if activists harp on about the damage done by alcohol. Most importantly, cannabis law reform activists are not arguing for alcohol prohibition, so there is little advantage in pointing out the damage caused by it (unless the activist is making the argument that the harms done by alcohol are considered acceptable by society and therefore cannabis ought to be accepted as well).

Whatever argument a cannabis law reform activist uses, it is important not to give the prohibitionist an avenue of attack. If the cannabis law reform activist demonstrates faulty logic even once, everything else they say will fall under suspicion. If in doubt it is best to stick to economic arguments, for the reason that, whatever moral values a person holds, few will object to having more money.

2. COUNTERING ARGUMENTS AGAINST CANNABIS LAW REFORM

Prohibition is the Common Thread

When arguing in favour of cannabis law reform, activists will hear many claims. Some of them have no basis in reality and can easily be dismissed with a reference to the facts of the situation. What is surprising is that a large number of the supposed problems that cannabis use causes are, in fact, problems caused by prohibition itself. Because the single strongest argument in favour of cannabis law reform is that prohibition simply doesn't work, it is best, whenever possible, to point out how the harms of cannabis use (when they actually exist) are caused by prohibition (and therefore would not be present if cannabis was regulated).

Cannabis law reform activists need to keep in mind that most of the arguments presented in favour of prohibition are so weak that, upon hearing them, the temptation is to burst out laughing. If you are debating cannabis law reform in front of a number of people it might be best to restrain these urges so as to not appear disrespectful. Of course these arguments are vicious, idiotic and in many cases obscene, but it is important to maintain an image that suggests the other side is not so much stupid as misinformed. Many people, even if they do not fully believe these arguments, will at least suspect that they might be true, and they will be more impressed by a calm but firm rebuttal than by sneering contempt.

Cannabis is a Gateway Drug

This argument is a staple of the drug warriors, and cannabis law reform activists will hear it time and time again, so it's important to be prepared for this one. The "gateway drug" theory claims that when people try cannabis they develop a desire to try other illegal drugs and soon become wretched slaves to heroin, krokodil and anything else they can get their hands on.

Like almost every other argument for prohibition, this is a total lie. Usage rates of cannabis far exceed those of heroin, methamphetamine or any other illicit drug, often by a factor of ten or more. If a recent drug use survey has been conducted in the activist's country, this would be an excellent time to mention it. Even if every single user of heroin or methamphetamine began to use those drugs after they first tried cannabis, the case for cannabis being a gateway drug would still be very weak. It could be pointed out here that the real gateway drugs are tobacco and alcohol.

If the activist does not have access to any hard data on the rates of heroin or methamphetamine use in their country, they could go on the counterattack. The fact is that in cases where cannabis use does lead to use of harder drugs, the only reason for this is that cannabis users must deal with the black market when trying to get hold of weed. Because cannabis is a poor choice of commodity for drug dealers (it smells and is worth relatively little if measured in either weight or volume), an incentive exists for them to get cannabis users hooked on something harder. This means that prohibition itself is responsible for many of the incidents of people becoming addicted to hard drugs.

Many people will not have looked at the issue from this perspective before and this approach will often cause them to reduce their opposition to cannabis law reform. If the activist detects that this is happening, the opportunity then exists to inform them about how the party policy will provide for the establishment of cannabis cafés where other drugs are banned (see Part Three of this book for a detailed discussion of this point).

People Would Use More Cannabis if it Was Legal

This argument is a tricky one from the perspective of a cannabis law reform activist, primarily because the activist is likely a cannabis user themselves and will see cannabis use as a good thing. This argument can only be made if coming from the perspective that cannabis use is harmful, and as a consequence there are two approaches that could be taken in response.

The first is to say, great! If people are smoking cannabis that keeps them off the booze and other hard drugs, and, considering the damage that those do, society wins by having a less dangerous alternative (see "It's an Alternative to Booze" in the previous section).

The second is to point out that the supposed wave of cannabis addicts that will result from law reform is a total myth. Most tellingly, this did not occur in the Netherlands after they relaxed cannabis prohibition. In fact, usage rates of both cannabis and a variety of other drugs went down: cannabis because it was no longer a "forbidden fruit" and the other drugs because people no longer had to go to criminal gangs who pushed them on people who only wanted to buy cannabis. Another blow to the myth is that rates of cannabis use are far higher in the USA, and in other prohibitionist countries, than they are in the Netherlands.

Legalisation Would Mean Young People Have Access to Cannabis

This argument, unlike most of the others for cannabis prohibition, is actually based on reasoning that appears logical. The current situation with alcohol is that someone who is underage, but who has a friend or older sibling who is not, can give that friend or relative some money and get that person to buy alcohol for them. The assumption made by prohibitionists is that, if cannabis is sold legally in coffee shops, people will buy it and give it to minors as they do with alcohol.

This may or may not happen if cannabis were legalised. But the truth of the matter is that the entire argument is a distraction from what happens under prohibition, which can be summed up in a simple phrase: gangs do not check for ID. The current unregulated market means that, in practice, minors need only to push a twenty dollar note through a hole in the wall of a tinny house and cannabis will come back in the other direction.

Like most of the other arguments in favour of cannabis prohibition, an activist who knows their material can go on the counterattack when this is made. If someone makes the claim that prohibition keeps cannabis out of the hands of the young, tell them and your audience that your opponent is, in fact, supporting a system in which anyone, regardless of vulnerability, can access it with no regulatory oversight whatsoever.

Prohibition Keeps Prices Higher, Thus Reducing Demand for Cannabis

This argument is based on basic economic principles. The price of cannabis is a function of its supply and its demand, and if prohibition can attack the supply side of the equation there will be less cannabis available, thereby driving up the price, which discourages its use.

Again, this argument affords an excellent chance to go on the counterattack. Even leaving aside the obvious counterpoint that a higher market price for cannabis will encourage people to produce it, the question has to be asked: where is the money going? It doesn't matter what the price of cannabis is if the money is all going into the hands of criminal gangs who do not even pay sales taxes on the product.

Legalisation of cannabis might reduce the price of the product, for the reason that large-scale cultivation would become possible and, as a consequence, economies of scale would drive down the price. It would also reduce the "risk premium" that is currently charged by cannabis dealers who must contend with the possibility that their inventory can be confiscated by the police. However, there is no reason why this increase in the profit margin could not be countered by taxation. The cannabis market in every country has settled on a standard price for the product; legalisation would create an opportunity for the government to raise revenue that could then be used on treatment for those users who were addicted, or on other social programs or tax cuts.

Cannabis Law Reform Would Invite Criminal Gangs to Operate in this Country

This is a classic bogeyman argument. Without the police force going into battle to win the War on Drugs, criminal gangs will flood here and bring cannabis with them, sucking money out of the country and destroying the people in it at the same time. If they don't enter from overseas, then the lower classes will form gangs to profit from the booming trade in cannabis sales.

The best response is to say that this is already happening, and that it would not be if the cannabis laws were reformed because people would be free to grow their own cannabis at home. If a person does not wish to grow their own, they would be able to buy it from a cannabis café At no point does the cannabis user need to come into contact with criminal gangs.

This argument can then be used to attack the prohibitionist position. It can be pointed out that the time in America's history most famous for gangs was when alcohol was prohibited, and the logical conclusion is that, as some gangs disappeared after alcohol law reform, so would other gangs disappear after cannabis law reform.

Cannabis Taxation Would Create a Huge Black Market for Cannabis

This argument is itself a counterargument, and to the

185

idea that cannabis law reform would result in considerable tax revenues. It states that any taxation applied to the sale of cannabis would mean that criminal gangs would still be able to undercut the market and flourish, so cannabis law reform would strengthen the gangs.

The first response to this is to point out that this has not happened with alcohol and tobacco. Even though it is legal to produce both of these drugs, people rarely do so. If people would rather buy something at a shop than produce it themselves, it is fair to say that they would not be inclined to go to a criminal gang.

The second response is to point out that the argument doesn't make economic sense. Any system of cannabis law reform would lower the production costs because there would be no risk of police interference and large-scale operations could spread start-up costs across a vast production run. Because production costs are lower, the gap between this and the production costs under prohibition can be made up for through taxation. This means that taxing cannabis would not increase the sale price, and therefore there would be no new market niche for the gangs to expand into.

Cannabis Use is Harmful

In most discussions on cannabis law reform this point is not even made as an argument; rather, it is an assumption that many people have. The government has made cannabis illegal, so the story goes, for our own good; people need to be protected from themselves.

Leaving aside the issue of how caging people helps them or anyone else, and the issue of how naive a person would have to be to believe that the government acts in its people's interests, the fact is that much of this harm is the direct result of prohibition.

No one can deny that smoking cannabis is bad for the lungs. This is a quality that cannabis shares with tobacco and any other organic substance that could be dried and smoked. However, there are other ways to consume cannabis that do not involve smoking bud, such as baking, or by using a water bong, an ice spottle or a vaporiser.

The problem with all of these methods of harm reduction is that they are usually illegal, and in most cases, more illegal than cannabis in dried flower form. Making cannabis oil and then putting it into a chocolate brownie is, in some jurisdictions, a higher grade of offence than possession of regular cannabis, and brings with it heavier penalties. Likewise, equipment that can be used to minimise the harm done by smoking is classed as "paraphernalia" and possession of it is itself a criminal offence.

The cannabis law reform activist can point out that it is the height of hypocrisy to declare something harmful at the same time as making measures to reduce that harm illegal.

A High Proportion of People With Substance Abuse Disorders Smoke Cannabis

If you examine the numbers of people who have been

diagnosed with substance abuse disorders, cannabis frequently ranks at or near the top of the list of drugs that some people are addicted to. This argument suggests that, because such a high proportion of substance abuse cases involve cannabis, cannabis must itself be an addictive and dangerous drug.

This argument is, of course, a total irrelevancy. All that matters is the total number of cannabis users who need help, not the proportion of cannabis users amongst the drug users who do seek help. The cannabis law reform activist can point this out, or they can retort that the high proportion of cannabis users reflects that failure of cannabis prohibition to keep the drug out of the hands of vulnerable people.

Cannabis Makes You Paranoid

Some people find that one of the effects of cannabis is to make them paranoid. This paranoia manifests itself in unwarranted suspicion of the people around them and fear that something terrible might happen. Because these feelings are unpleasant, the argument is made that cannabis ought to be made illegal in order to prevent them.

The truth is that people who smoke cannabis don't feel paranoid because of the nature of the drug, but because of prohibition itself. Anyone who smokes a joint, even in the privacy of their own home, knows that there is a possibility that the police can enter their house, drag them off and lock them in a cage. On top of this, there is the chance that any other person who is aware that someone else possesses cannabis can call the police and

treated like tobacco, it would be either manufactured by companies who would be prohibited from adding such drugs to the product or it would be grown at home by people who would not lace their own product.

Cannabis Causes Schizophrenia

Drug warriors are fond of referencing the infamous study of Swedish conscripts that appeared to suggest that young people who smoked cannabis in their youth were many times more likely to develop schizophrenia later in their life. Leaving aside the methodology of the study, and whether such a fanatically anti-cannabis country such as Sweden could be trusted to provide an honest investigation into such a matter, a simple examination of the reality shows that there is little, if any, connection between the two.

Cannabis usage rates have increased markedly since the 1950's, at which time the drug was little known to most people, and even then their opinions were mostly based on films such as *Reefer Madness*. In recent years, youth cannabis use in many countries is almost as high as it is for alcohol, and yet diagnosed rates of schizophrenia have not increased. If cannabis use caused schizophrenia there would not only be a documented increase in schizophrenia when cannabis use increased within a population, but also a higher rate of schizophrenia in countries that smoked more cannabis. Neither is the case.

In some cases, cannabis use has been connected to a number of emergency room visits because of people freaking out. Again, this is a problem with prohibition

191

because it is impossible to get any truthful information about the effect of cannabis to high school students owing to the tsunami of propaganda coming in the other direction. If it is hammered into people's heads that they will freak out and go insane from smoking cannabis, this is indeed what will happen, regardless of the psychoactive effects of cannabis.

In any case, the causal link between cannabis and onset of schizophrenia is not the issue. The status quo involves people at risk of mental illness being arrested, thrown into a cage and then dragged in front of a judge, who will then usually impose further restrictions to that person's liberty and social standing. It is therefore not difficult to see how the system of prohibition is worse for people's mental health than the alternative.

We Don't Want to Send the Wrong Message to the Youth

This argument will come up again and again, for, although it is possibly the single most dishonest and vacuous argument ever given, it appears to be effective. It is hard to argue against this because it is not clear what the message is. Presumably the message is that, if a person wants to have a good time, they would be better off drinking alcohol, or taking no drugs at all.

If this argument is given in a debate on cannabis law reform, the activist ought to ask what the message actually is and go from there. This will force the prohibitionist to make a more concrete claim which can then be demolished in line with the counter arguments previously given in this section.

If you have read through this handbook up until this point, you might suspect what the message really is. It is "we own you", and this mentality is at the core of all efforts to prohibit the use and sale of cannabis. What makes cannabis law reform difficult is that a large section of the voting age population does not have a problem with this. Cannabis prohibition is, of course, at its base, a philosophy of evil, and no arguments, however well researched or articulated, will overcome this.

Cannabis Makes People Impotent

It has to be conceded that this argument, as dishonest as it is, is very clever: a man may or may not care about health problems such as lung cancer or brain damage, but any kind of problem with his penis will command his full attention. It belongs in the same category as the claim that smoking cannabis will make you gay, which is to say that it is a total lie, but one that seeks to persuade on a purely emotional level.

Of course, anyone who has smoked cannabis and then had sex will attest that not only is this not true, but it is actually the reverse of the truth. Stoned sex is great and there really is nothing like it. Any male smoker can attest to the heightened penile sensitivity that follows smoking cannabis. The documentary *Super High Me*, in which the comedian Doug Benson smoked large amounts of cannabis for thirty days, revealed that Benson's sperm count actually increased after the thirty days of indulgence.

Perhaps the best counter to this argument is to point out

193

that even if smoking cannabis did affect blood flow to the penis and thereby produced erectile dysfunction, it is not anywhere near as bad as the "whisky dick" that alcohol is famous for.

Cannabis Turns People into Unemployed Losers

Part of winning the battle against cannabis prohibition is winning the war of perception. Like it or not, there will always be people who know someone who is both unemployed and a cannabis user, and in the minds of some people this is sufficient evidence for the dreaded "amotivational syndrome." There are two ways to argue against this point.

The first is to point out that there is no obvious connection between smoking cannabis and losing one's job, or staying unemployed. People were unemployed and lazy long before cannabis came onto the scene, and most drug abusing welfare recipients are alcoholics, not cannabis users. Until the global financial crisis of 2008, usage rates for cannabis were often higher than the unemployment rates in certain countries, which means that, even if every single unemployed person was a cannabis user, there would still be cannabis users who were in full-time employment.

The second is less intellectual but probably more effective. Simply ask "what about Sir Richard Branson?" Branson, one of Britain's wealthiest men, is an avowed cannabis user and has spoken out against cannabis prohibition, citing, amongst other things, the fact that it is a gigantic waste of money that achieves nothing. It is not easy to make the case that smoking cannabis helped to make Branson as wealthy as he is, but it does not appear to have harmed him any. If smoking cannabis does not prevent a man from becoming a multibillionaire, it is difficult to argue that it would seriously harm the chances of anyone wishing to merely work full-time.

Once People Get into Cannabis, They Get into Crime

Many people will have observed the common pattern of a young person getting into cannabis and soon afterwards expanding into crime. The logical error is in assuming that it was the cannabis that caused that person to develop a criminal attitude, and therefore cannabis should stay illegal in order to keep crime down. There are several ways to argue against this point.

The first is, as ever, to point out that this is a problem with prohibition and not with cannabis. If cannabis is illegal, people must buy it from criminals. Through coming into contact with criminals people become tempted to commit crimes for money, especially if the gains from these crimes can be traded immediately for drugs. The cannabis law reform activist can point out that reform would destroy this chain of behaviour, because people would no longer have to solicit goods from criminals.

Another way is to point out that making cannabis illegal has the result that people who smoke it sometimes decide that laws are stupid and need not be respected or obeyed. If cannabis were legal, people would no longer think this.

**Cannabis is Much Stronger Than It Used to Be, and
Therefore More Dangerous**

Often a cannabis law reform activist will read a
newspaper report in which a police officer claims that
modern cannabis is extra dangerous because artificial
selection techniques have been used to breed a plant that
has ten, twenty or even thirty times as much THC in it as
it used to have. Cannabis growers have, so we're told,
recklessly bred this "superskunk" in response to demand
for a drug that can take people higher than ever before,
and this serves as the background to the then predictable
claim that the hospital emergency services are becoming
overwhelmed with the resultant casualties.

Because the prohibitionist mentality believes that the
THC in cannabis directly causes mental illness, it stands
to (their) reason that, the higher the THC component, the
more mental illness will be caused. For this reason, both
police and the public need to be especially vigilant about
any cannabis on the streets and a stance of zero tolerance
should be adopted, invariably "for the children." It is this
author's contention that anyone who advocates to take
freedoms away from adults while using the phrase "for
the children" ought to be made to parade around the
streets wearing a dunce cap, but because this is not
realistic it is better to examine the scientific reality of
this claim.

The botanical fact is that there is an upper limit to how
much stronger cannabis could possibly be. The cannabis
plant must grow from a seedling to a plant with a stem,
and from there grow branches and leaves and finally
flowers. Apart from the flowers, there is very little THC

in the rest of the plant, and if the THC percentage of the flowers alone was at the maximum possible point beyond which the plant would no longer be viable, it might be at around 25%. A plant, however it is bred and grown, cannot go past the point where its THC level renders the rest of the plant unable to function. At the other end, cannabis with a THC level of 1% or lower is called hemp, because for all its farming and industrial uses, smoking it will only give you a headache. Even the weakest cannabis that is sold and smoked for pleasure has around 2.5% THC, and varieties of around 8-10% THC provide the bulk of which is sold to recreational users. Knowing these figures, it becomes obvious that the supposed increase in THC behind the latest moral panic is impossible. Even if all weed "back in the day" was 3% THC, it would reach its upper bounds at 25% THC and therefore never be more than eight times stronger than its predecessors. This comparison is even after cherry-picking the weakest of the older cannabis strains against the most psychoeffective modern ones.

People Shouldn't Have to Pay for Cannabis Users' Healthcare

This argument is a common one nowadays, and will probably become more common as time passes. It's essentially a selfish argument, and it runs like this: "I don't care what people do in their own homes, as long as I don't have to pay for the health costs of it. If cannabis was legalised, I'd have to pay for all the addicts and psych cases that it caused."

The counter to this argument is simple: cannabis would be taxed at a rate that provided revenues equal to the

197

health care costs caused by law reform. The truth is that cannabis users would love the chance to counter the perception that they are bludging, thieving parasites, and if they could pay taxes on legal weed, they would.

The argument can be extended to point out that many people would, if given the legal option, pursue courses of medical marijuana that might replace courses of more expensive medicines otherwise paid for by insurance or government money. The natural endpoint of this extension is that overall health care costs would actually be lower if cannabis was legalised, because this would allow a cheap medicine onto the market.

Cannabis Use Must Be Discouraged for the Good of Society

Because one of the most common arguments put forward in favour of cannabis law reform is that people should have ownership rights to their own bodies, and therefore the right to decide for themselves what goes in it, one of the most common prohibitionist replies is to say that people do not have the right to make society pay for the consequences of that person's cannabis use.

The counterargument to this is that society already is paying for the consequences of that person's drug use, and those expenses are far greater because of cannabis prohibition. All taxpayers lose out when cannabis users have to go through the court and the prison system, and all members of a family lose out when one of them is taken away for a cannabis offence. If it is important that society not be burdened by wasted tax money, why have cannabis prohibition when it costs so much?

It can also be pointed out that society benefits from the positive effects of cannabis use. People get to relax and have a good time and do it with far fewer financial, criminal or health problems than with alcohol.

The Majority Does Not Want Cannabis Law Reform

This argument is an appeal to the legitimacy of the herd. It states that, because there is not majority support for cannabis law reform, it is right to keep it illegal because this is how democracies operate. There are at least three counters to this argument.

The first is that it isn't necessarily true. Prohibitionists will claim that the majority is against cannabis even when there are polls suggesting a desire for reform - this, of course, leaves them wide open if proof of such a poll can be given. Although the cannabis law reform activist can find themselves working in an area where the majority do support prohibition, this does not mean that all groups within that population support it. The young, in particular, are almost always more cannabis friendly than their elders. No matter what the results of any poll are, the cannabis law reform activist can always point out that the tide has been moving towards reform for decades now, and that it is therefore sure to win after enough time passes.

The second is to point out that the majority may not oppress a minority in any democracy worthy of the name. Democracies (generally) do not exterminate minority groups within their borders, even if the majority of the population is bloodthirsty enough to support this. The cannabis law reform activist can ask

199

any prohibitionist who makes the "majority rules" argument how old they are, and then ask if they'd be okay with everyone who is not that age voting to put people of that age in prison. No one would agree, although the argument is as logical as the argument that cannabis users can be oppressed merely because the majority wishes it to be so.

The third is to point out that many people have absolutely no experience of cannabis or of cannabis users and as a result they form their opinions on information from biased sources. Going all the way back to *Reefer Madness*, the official word on cannabis has been much harsher than the reality. Many old people will not have seen *Reefer Madness* but will have formed their opinions based on conversations with people who had. This counterargument is to say that, if people were told the truth about cannabis, a majority of them would support law reform.

I Know Someone Who Smoked Cannabis and Went Crazy

This argument might just sound silly, but it's amazing how many times it gets brought up. Every prohibitionist seems to know one person who was the pillar of their community but who was brought low by the demon weed. Invariably that person was bright, a bit sensitive and naive, and what is not said is that they possessed all of the classic signs of developing a psychotic illness before they smoked any cannabis. What is not mentioned is how many other cannabis smokers that person knows who aren't going crazy, nor the people going crazy who aren't smoking cannabis.

One way to counter this is to simply point out that knowing one person who smoked cannabis and went crazy says nothing of the overall situation in the world, and that a single datapoint is not evidence of any wider trend. If the prohibitionist insists that there are many others who have wound up in a similar situation, the cannabis law reform activist can express the hope that the fear of authority caused by prohibition did not discourage them from getting mental health care.

Perhaps the best way to depower this argument is to show concern for the person affected and the treatment they received. Ask if they got help for their breakdown, and whether this help got them back on their feet. The cannabis law reform activist could point out that others in this situation do not get the help they need to recover because to do so would require admitting that they have broken the law.

If It Ain't Broke, Why Fix It?

This argument states that, as bad as cannabis prohibition may be, as there is even the slightest possibility that law reform could make some problems worse, we ought to stick to prohibition. It is really the argument of a person who is almost persuaded that cannabis law reform is a superior option to prohibition, because it has nearly conceded everything that must be conceded before someone can become a supporter.

The strangest thing about this argument is that it could more effectively be used by those arguing for cannabis law reform. There were no major problems with cannabis use in society before prohibition was brought in, and there are major problems now. Cannabis law reform would actually be a move back to the way things were, and even the way things had been for as many as 5,000 years.

It has to be kept in mind that people who do not use cannabis may not see the system as broken because they are not at the sharp end of it. People like this are best persuaded by using economic arguments.

The Criminal Justice System is a Path to Treatment

This argument contends that cannabis prohibition is a good thing because it allows for mental health services to reach people who they should be helping, but who would have been ignored if not arrested for a cannabis offence.

This argument only makes sense if there are cannabis users out there who walk a tightrope between being too mentally ill to function but mentally healthy enough to (so far) evade detection. The activist may wish to invite the audience to consider the moral aspects of using armed police to arrest and imprison mentally ill people, but it is not advisable to give any ground to the prohibitionists' attempts to label cannabis users as mentally ill.

If the audience believes that the criminal justice system is a good way to treat cannabis dependency issues, then they are probably right-wing, which means the cannabis law reform activist could attack from the far side of that right wing, and make a libertarian argument. Try telling the audience that people in this country should have the freedom to seek treatment should they decide that is has become necessary, and that this is only possible if the cannabis laws are reformed.

Cannabis Law Reform Would Weaken Efforts to Combat Drugged Driving

Prohibitionists are keen to point out that a large number of people are caught driving a motor vehicle with "cannabis in their system." Statistics are thrown about showing that many of the drivers involved in fatal road accidents "tested positive" for cannabis. The implication is that, if cannabis law reform were to be enacted, there would be more people smoking cannabis and therefore more fatal car accidents and injuries.

The first counterargument is to say that cannabis use does not tend to rise when cannabis law reform is enacted. This is a strong response but many people simply do not believe this is true, because it goes against common sense. It cannot be repeated enough that the Netherlands has one of the lowest rates of cannabis use in Europe (and presumably, therefore, one of the lowest rates of car accidents caused solely by cannabis use) despite their relatively liberal cannabis policy.

The second counterargument is to mention that cannabis can show up in a test several weeks after it was taken, and because cannabis is only effective for a few hours, most of the people who test positive for cannabis were in no way under its psychoactive influence, let alone too impaired to drive.

Care must be taken if the activist comes up against this

argument, because it's possible to counter it and still lose. This happens when the activist appears indifferent to those impacted by drugged driving.

We Don't Want People Coming to Work Stoned

This is a tricky argument, because it could be made to sow fear or it could be the result of an honest but inaccurate idea of what prohibition is about. It states that cannabis should be illegal because of the possibility that people will come to work stoned. For some reason, nurses are the example usually given, perhaps because they have the most responsibility for the least pay.

A good counter is to point out that irresponsible people are irresponsible people, and there is no-one who would come to work stoned that has not already done so drunk. No-one wants nurses coming to work stoned any more than drunk or drowsy on prescription medication. In any case, because cannabis is easily available to anyone with any determination, the hypothetical naughty nurse could well be coming to work stoned anyway. At least after law reform she'd know what strength THC she had smoked.

Perhaps a more reassuring counter is to say that, even though cannabis should be legal, businesses would still have the right to send anyone home if their state of mind could be dangerous to themselves or to their workmates.

Drugs Are Bad, Mmmmmkay?

One of the lows of any cannabis activist's career is listening to someone disagree so violently with you that they launch into a spittle-flecked rant about heroin, cocaine, crack, meth and any other drug but cannabis. Avoiding this is the main reason why it is a good idea to not use the phrase "alcohol and drugs." Unfortunately, in the minds of many people there are two categories of psychoactive substances: alcohol and bad stuff. Trying to argue with people who think like this is futile, because it is "common sense" that drugs are bad and that is all there is to it.

In some ways, being a cannabis law reform activist is like being an explorer trying to persuade some unsophisticated tribe that sacrificing virgins will not affect the whims of the thunder god. Given time, every cannabis law reform activist will hear arguments for prohibition that are so grossly irrational that even a monkey would laugh to hear them.

In a sense this is a very good thing, because it simplifies the strategy of the activist. Stupid people will not be convinced by reason, so when one is encountered it is time to use any and all emotional arguments whether they are known or made up on the spot.

On Balance, Prohibition is Better

This weasely way of arguing comes after the cannabis law reform activist has scored several points. A prohibitionist might use it in any situation where they are losing, and will usually cite "common sense" to back themselves up. The tactic is to concede some or all of the points made thus far, and then to claim that, because of some nebulous reason, prohibition is still better "on balance." The reasons are inevitably things that cannot be quantified, such as moral decay.

Perhaps the best answer is to say "Things aren't balanced - it's costing us a billion dollars a year." This is not an entirely logical counter but the original statement is fallacious anyway.

Refuse to let any prohibitionist cloud the issue with vagaries and doubt. If they try, bring the debate straight back to the facts.

The Moral Argument

This is one of the more difficult arguments to counter, because it appeals to a side of people that is not rational and will not be changed by an intellectual response. It contends that cannabis use is, in and of itself, immoral, and because it is immoral it should be prohibited by law. Usually nothing is said about using any other method to persuade people that cannabis use could be harmful to them - it is all about the punishment. Cannabis users are sinners, and must be purified by suffering.

The real difficulty with countering this argument is that those who have made it may have a very different set of moral values to those arguing for cannabis law reform, and the activist may not have the time to perform a detailed psychoanalysis on such matters. The best counterargument might be to declare that cannabis prohibition is actually more immoral, and hope that the audience agrees.

The audience might believe that locking someone up for an act that harmed no-one is immoral because it is cruel, or that spending all this money on a losing battle is wasteful, or that having a crusade against cannabis when there are far greater concerns in the world is rash and foolish. The activist might have to consider their audience before declaring that there are worse examples of moral failure than cannabis law reform.

The Ultimate Counterargument

This is a very simple one, but it is effective. In all of the jurisdictions where cannabis prohibition has been relaxed, none of the predictions of doom have come to pass. The best way to make this counterargument as effective as possible is to stay informed. You can counter many of the predictions of societal collapse by simply saying "It didn't happen in the Netherlands." Other places in the world are experimenting with cannabis law reform, and these examples can also be used.

The prohibitionist will appeal to the "common sense" of the audience, which is putting a nice spin on what is actually a collection of received wisdom that is yet to be corrected. Common sense will tell people a lot of things, but the facts, less common though they be, do not support them. Cannabis law reform would mean all the young people will smoke it? Didn't happen in the Netherlands. Cannabis law reform would mean our streets are flooded with heroin addicts? Didn't happen in Portugal. Limited home grow would lead to people selling cannabis to schoolkids on their way home? Didn't happen in the Australian Capital Territory.

This argument will need to be made often, because if the prohibitionist feels they are losing an argument they will try and introduce as much uncertainty into it as possible. Sometimes this line of argumentation will surprise people, as a lot of people do not know that cannabis law reform has succeeded in some places. If this occurs, it is a good time to press on and elaborate on the other ways these examples of cannabis law reform have made life better.

PART THREE: TAKING IT TO THE TRENCHES

With a movement assembled and the ability to win on financial, logistical and intellectual fronts established, all that remains is getting to the front lines. There is more than one way to fight for cannabis law reform. The first part of this handbook focused on building a movement, the second on training it and this third part will focus on the actual fighting.

In this sense it is best to think of an election as a great battle, where warlords, kings and statesmen come to do battle for the mantle and the mace. In a democratic system, their power is represented in the vote count. This means that every election is, for its candidates, an attempt to summon the power of the voters into a force capable of exerting its will on the national stage.

The fun part about electioneering is that the country goes into election mode. It is never easier to get free media attention for the cannabis cause, or to get people to pay attention to the argument for law reform, than at election time. People will stop and listen to a candidate speak when they would ignore them for a lunatic at any other time.

A cannabis law reform movement can fight in the courts as well as it can at the ballot box. It is difficult to give legal advice in this handbook because the cannabis law reform movement covers so many different jurisdictions. Instead, some general strategic principles are outlined.

Basic Debating Strategy

At all times you must ensure that you frame the debate. Your rights are under debate, so you frame the debate in your terms. The prohibitionists will try and get you bogged down in trivial detail so that your core message is weakened. Do not fall for this. The core message is that people have the right to use cannabis, and this message can be asserted at any time.

The most basic strategy is the one two punch. Declare that the best legal approach would be one of harm reduction, and then argue that cannabis law reform is less harmful. This is important because many of the arguments put forward in favour of cannabis prohibition are blatant sophistry. With a frame of "harm reduction," you rule out of the debate moral arguments, appeals to common sense, appeals to tradition, and many other irrationalities that may still persuade a naive audience.

Part of this is not allowing a prohibitionist to weasel away when they are on the losing side of a point. If they do not tell the truth, hammer them on it. Let the audience know that their other points must be under a cloud of suspicion owing to previous lies.

If You Have an Open Goal, Kick the Ball In

The prohibitionist machine may be large, well-funded, aggressive and loud, but it is also clumsy, stupid and full of weak points. As it lurches through the media landscape it reveals, to anyone watching, vulnerabilities at which it can be struck. Never let an opportunity go to waste. Any weak point might be discovered and reinforced before it can be attacked.

For example, if there is a report in a local newspaper about a fourteen-year old getting suspended from school because cannabis was discovered in their backpack, the cannabis law reform movement must take the points on offer. The local branch President should contact everyone in the branch and suggest to write a letter to the editor pointing out the flaws in the prohibitionist model, and the superiority of the law reform model. Inform the public that gangs happily sell cannabis to fourteen-year olds, and cannabis cafés do not.

It is true that it is better to campaign actively rather than reactively, but it is also true that reactive force is easier to organise. If a cannabis law reform movement cannot generate at least a few hundred letters whenever it is attacked then it will appear very weak to anyone considering voting for it.

Keep Your Information Fresh

One of the good things about fighting for cannabis law reform is that public opinion is slowly but inexorably moving in its favour. A consequence is that it is easy to find reports in the media of a new study, or an opinion from a former judge or law enforcement officer in favour of reform. For example, a month before this handbook was published, Judge Richard A. Posner of the Seventh Circuit U.S. Court of Appeals stated that he saw little difference between cannabis and tobacco and that it was "absurd to be criminalizing possession or use or distribution of marijuana."

There are often reports like this in the media, and if a cannabis law reform activist can reference the most recent one it will create the impression that public opinion is turning in favour of reform (which it is). This will also give the cannabis law reform activist an advantage if one of their opponents references an old study that has since been debunked.

1. AN EXAMPLE PARTY POLICY

If an activist or party official succeeds in making a person receptive to the cannabis law reform message, that person will inevitably ask "What would you do if you were in power?" Essentially the second part of this handbook is all about persuading someone that cannabis prohibition is a failure; this part is about persuading them that the policy of the cannabis law reform party would be an improvement.

This part of the handbook does not describe the official policy of any cannabis law reform party, although its core points are based on the policy of the Aotearoa Legalise Cannabis Party, which has fought for cannabis law reform in New Zealand since 1996. Copying an existing party's policy would be impractical owing to the different and changing local conditions that various cannabis law reform movements will encounter. It is also impossible because different cannabis law reform parties will have different core values and therefore an unique emphasis on their choice of policy.

It is, however, an example of a comprehensive party policy that covers all the areas that cannabis law reform might impact on. No matter how strongly a person agrees that cannabis prohibition is a monstrous failure, they will only vote for a cannabis law reform party if that party can clearly present a better way of doing things, and if that party can explain how this way of doing things is better for that particular voter.

When presenting a party policy there are two major

213

considerations. The first is how aggressive the language should be. Politics is cut-throat and for this reason the language in this part is more inflammatory than in the previous two, but activists elsewhere might choose to tone it down or even make it sharper, depending on their objectives. The second is that the party policy ought to be presented in a fashion so that the least objectionable policies come first.

In this part of the handbook, the hypothetical cannabis law reform party is called the Cannabis Party, which may, of course, be changed to suit local conditions.

The Twenty-Six Point Plan

One way of presenting a policy document for a cannabis law reform party is to produce a plan. The policy in this section is presented as if it were a twenty-six point plan; one point for every letter of the alphabet. Depending on local conditions, a cannabis law reform movement could use all or some of the following points.

The way to use them is to present them as a list of demands. There is no argument here, and these points only have counterpoints in the context of negotiation. The idea is to present the most aggressive written document short of a declaration of violent intent, with the implied demand that the establishment will make concessions to the cannabis culture for every point not granted.

If the plan is presented correctly, anyone reading it will understand that cannabis users are aware of the degree to which their rights are being violated, and that we intend to restore every single one of them.

A. An Immediate Ceasefire

Cannabis Party policy demands an immediate moratorium on arrests for any cannabis related activity apart from supplying cannabis to minors. From the date of the moratorium onward, police will no longer have the right to arrest or detain people for cannabis related offences, nor to search them or their property on the pretext of having smelt cannabis.

B. Throw Out All Cases in Progress

Cannabis Party policy demands that all procedures for cannabis offences currently in progress in the court system, apart from supplying cannabis to minors, are to be thrown out.

C. Release the Prisoners

Cannabis Party policy demands that any person currently serving a custodial sentence for a cannabis offence, apart from supplying cannabis to minors, is to be released without delay.

D. Victims to be Compensated

Cannabis Party policy demands that, because the only crime with cannabis is prohibition, those who have been affected by it must be compensated for the violation of their human rights that they experienced. Anyone who was forced to pay a fine for a cannabis offence is to be reimbursed at interest. Anyone who was imprisoned as a result of being charged with a cannabis offence is to receive $1,000 for every day that they spent imprisoned. Any assets that have been seized by government officials as a result of a cannabis offence are to be returned.

E. Criminal Records to be Expunged

Cannabis Party policy demands that any existing criminal record relating to a cannabis offence is to be expunged. No official record will be retained of that person having committed that offence. People who previously had cannabis convictions on their criminal record will be under no legal obligation to declare this to anyone.

F. Provision to be Made for Industrial Hemp

Cannabis Party policy demands that all legal restrictions on the cultivation and sale of hemp products be removed. Provision must be made for the establishment of a nationwide, full-scale hemp industry.

G. Market for Personal Use of Cannabis to be Regulated

Cannabis Party policy demands that the personal use of cannabis be regulated in a manner similar to tobacco and alcohol.

H. Research into Cannabis Issues to be Funded

Cannabis Party policy demands that funds be directed to the study of cannabis issues in our society. The Cannabis Party will devote some of our billion dollar windfall to sponsoring university research, keeping our best brains in the country and working on improving the lives of our own citizens.

I. Cannabis Cafés to be Established

Cannabis Party policy demands that provision be made to establish cannabis cafés in this country. The cannabis cafés will operate on the same model that has succeeded in the Netherlands. Cannabis cafés will operate under certain restrictions to ensure that their impact on society is minimised.

J. Truthful Cannabis Education to be Given at Schools

Cannabis Party policy demands an end to the propaganda spewed at high school students about the supposed dangers of cannabis use. Any drug education that is given to high school students must emphasise that the overwhelming majority of drug deaths are caused by alcohol and tobacco.

K. Rehabilitation Centres to be Funded

Cannabis Party policy demands that some of the revenue from the taxation of cannabis be used for the rehabilitation of people with substance abuse disorders. Because many people who need help have been deterred by prohibition, it is essential that we make provision for those who have been neglected.

L. The Phrase "Alcohol and Drugs" to be Removed from the Government's Vocabulary

Cannabis Party policy demands that the Government be honest to the people, and stop using the phrase "alcohol and drugs" as if alcohol was not a drug. No official Government publication may use the phrase.

M. Limited Home Grow to be Legalised

Cannabis Party policy demands that every adult have the right to grow cannabis for personal use in their own home. Every adult would be allowed to grow up to six cannabis plants for personal use.

N. Cannabis Advocacy Agency to be Established to Deprogram People from Propaganda

Cannabis Party policy demands that some of the revenue from the taxation of cannabis be used for a national truth campaign that seeks to overturn the stereotypes of cannabis users that the Government has established over recent decades.

O. Cannabis Use to be Added to Bill of Rights Act

Cannabis Party policy demands that a person's choice to use cannabis be exempt from discrimination. If a person's cannabis use does not affect their job performance, it may not be used to refuse a person a job or to fire a person from a job they have.

P. Adults to Have the Right to Gift Cannabis

Cannabis Party policy demands that adults have the right to gift cannabis to other adults for their personal use without being charged with supplying an illegal substance.

Q. People Have the Right to Medicinal Cannabis

Cannabis Party policy demands that people have the right to use cannabis or cannabis products for medicinal aims. Whatever a person's belief on the recreational or industrial uses of cannabis, denying its use as a medicine is an inhumanity that must stop immediately.

R. Uses of Medicinal Cannabis to be Researched

Cannabis Party policy demands that the neglect of the therapeutic potential of cannabis be immediately addressed. To this end, some of the revenue from the taxation of cannabis must be used to sponsor research into medical uses of cannabis.

S. The Environmental Benefits of Cannabis to be Assessed

Cannabis Party policy demands that an environmental impact assessment be made comparing the crops of the status quo with hemp.

T. Job Training for those Displaced by Law Reform

Cannabis Party policy demands that no-one suffer from the change to cannabis regulation. This means that some of the revenue generated by cannabis taxation must be used to retrain police officers, gang members and others who earned a living from cannabis prohibition. Some police officers previously tasked with cannabis prohibition can be assigned to aggressively police the sale of cannabis to minors.

U. Drug Dogs To Be Humanely Retired

Cannabis Party policy demands that all drug dogs trained to bark upon detection of cannabis be retired from the police force. If homes for them cannot be found, they are to be looked after until the end of their natural lives from revenue generated by cannabis taxation.

V. Seized Assets to be Returned

Cannabis Party policy demands that any asset seized in relation to the prosecution of a cannabis law be returned to its rightful owner, or compensation be paid equal to the value of the stolen assets.

W. (Optional) Open a Ministry of Cannabis Affairs

Cannabis Party policy demands that some of the revenue from cannabis taxation be used to establish a Ministry of Cannabis Affairs. The purpose of this Ministry is to establish who made cannabis illegal, who kept it illegal, and who wants to make it illegal in the future.

X. (Optional) Rescind the Single Convention on Narcotics

Cannabis Party policy demands that our nation withdraw from the Single Convention on Narcotics on the grounds that its provisions are against human rights.

Y. (Optional) Legalise Other Drugs

Cannabis Party policy demands that provision be made for other illegal drugs to follow a similar path to law reform as cannabis.

Z. Your Issue Here

If the party has decided to at least flirt with issues not directly related to cannabis, one or more of these could be added to the plan. To do so may be a concession that the party is not a single-issue one, but it might not. If the pamphlet is produced for a small market, Issue Z could be a community project that has stalled through lack of funding and could be paid for with revenue from cannabis taxation. If it can be determined how much money cannabis prohibition costs each person a year, this figure can be multiplied by how many people are in an area. Anything less than that total cost has the potential to be a pet project that is sponsored by the cannabis law reform movement.

A quick scan of the recent letters to the editor of the local newspaper will tell you what the issues on the minds of the people there are, and usually one of these issues will be a lack of funding for something. If the something lacking funding is a public good or service, then you have an issue that few will disagree upon (and a solution that no-one else is offering).

It is probably best if the issue to be taken up relates to health, housing, education, infrastructure, or some other public good or service, and not any other political cause. The reason for this is that taking up another political cause will alienate some of your voters. The cannabis issue is controversial enough as it is, and it does not need to be associated with another "radical" policy.

2. RUNNING A CAMPAIGN

This section is much smaller than it deserves to be, but only because much of what belongs in it is covered in the first part of this book. The most important thing to remember is that an election campaign grows with every member signed up, even if this happens years before election day. Therefore, membership, fundraising and media work done at any time since the last election counts as effort towards the next campaign.

Having said this, there are some considerations that apply to a campaign only in the final weeks. These will be covered in this section of the handbook.

It's a Marathon, Not a Sprint

Although the minute-by-minute pressures of an election campaign can be intense at times, the drama lasts for weeks and the most effective time to put effort in is right at the end. For these reasons it is best to view an election campaign as a long march through unfamiliar territory.

Ego depletion theory tells us that the brain behaves as if it has a reserve of energy that can be depleted after too much thought. If a person has faced a number of intellectually challenging tasks in a short time period, their brain may lose some of its ability to deal with what is going on.

Like sporting events, the winners of political campaigns are the ones who did their preparation in advance. If the party has powerful systems in place, if these systems do not break down, if all necessary information is readily accessible, and if party communication is good, activists will be able to use their minds more efficiently and will be fresher at the end.

The beginning of the election campaign is when the party starts expending resources instead of gathering them. The election campaign is the part of the marathon where the runners enter the stadium and do one lap. This reveals the secret: the winner is already decided, and it is whoever has prepared the best.

World War I or World War II?

Although World Wars One and Two were fought relatively close together, the tactics were often very different, and reflect two different strategies for victory. World War I was characterised by attacks along a line, with the attacker seeking to overwhelm the enemy. World War II was characterised by the Blitzkrieg concept of the schwerpunkt, in which one point in the line was hit with as much force as possible until it broke, at which point the attack would pile through.

A World War I style election campaign would involve running candidates in every possible seat, and a World War II style campaign would involve piling all resources into winning one seat and building from there.

In practice, a party might have to find a balance between these extremes, which might mean running candidates in every seat but only seriously funding a handful of them. It is good to run high-profile campaigns, because winning any electoral seat would be a triumph, and running a large number of low-profile campaigns allows the party to see which electorates have potential.

Selecting a Campaign Manager

For a cannabis law reform party to run an effective electoral campaign, it needs to task one person with overall authority for planning and executing that campaign. This can be a person from the Executive (the Press Secretary might be a good choice), or the membership, or even from outside.

The advantage with using a person from the outside is that they will not be involved in all of the petty squabbles that regularly afflict political parties. They have not been party to the backstabbing and the alliance building, and they might not even care who is in control of the party. Their objective is simply to help the party win the election. The disadvantage with using a person from the outside is that it is very difficult to gauge their loyalty to the movement. People take money from others to sabotage election campaigns, and it is wise to be wary of this possibility. There is also the possibility that a manager from the outside will not have the necessary status to properly inspire action.

The advantage with using a person from the Executive is that they will know a lot about how the movement works and who is in it. This will mean that they can more effectively bring resources to bear and use them. The disadvantage is that Executive members generally have a lot to do anyway, and because it is crucial that the party survive the election in order to fight the next one, they cannot easily take on an entire extra and new role.

For the above reasons it is possibly best that the Campaign Manager comes from the non-Executive body of the membership. This will make it possible for the Executive to choose someone who knows enough about how the party functions to direct it, and for a regular member to take an active and important role in the success of the party.

Special Considerations of a Campaign Manager

If the Campaign Manager is not appointed from the Executive, they may find that they are not aware of many party traditions, conventions and practices. This means that they have to get involved with a certain degree of caution. Election time or not, the other members of the Executive may not let a Campaign Manager assume any authority that isn't theirs.

The lists kept by the Membership Secretary (see "Extraordinary Considerations of the Membership Secretary") are of extreme value to the Campaign Manager at election time. Should the Campaign Manager need to encourage some volunteer action in a certain place and time, the lists will tell them who is active in that area, what skills they have and how helpful they have been in the past.

The Campaign Manager has one considerable advantage when it comes to motivating people to volunteer at election time. Because there is usually no position of Campaign Manager, any member getting communication from one will understand that it is a special situation that might require special action. Related to this, the Campaign Manager will need to project a sense of urgency at all times. This is important to inspire other members to take action. Given the pressures of the election, this should come naturally.

Selecting a Candidate

There are two ways of selecting a candidate: they can be chosen by the party Executive or they can be elected by the membership of the branch or chapter. In most cases there will be no conflict between the two, because the Executive will understand that the will of the members of a branch must be respected.

The party membership has little need for advice on who they should select as a candidate. Their collective will and intelligence ought to be enough to ensure that they put forward as a leader a person who can skilfully represent both them and the movement.

The national body may wish to have veto rights over a candidate in case there is a rogue element or in case the election of that candidate was somehow improperly conducted. The party should not allow a candidate to run if their candidacy makes the party less likely to win.

Special Considerations of a Candidate

Any candidate for a cannabis law reform party must be aware that running for public office invites a lot of attention. All manner of people will call and many of them will be referred to the candidate by an officer within the party. This entails an unusual lack of privacy, which is normal for people in the public eye but may not have been for the candidate.

The candidate must not only get used to this attention but revel in it. Every passer-by affords an opportunity to snare a vote. Any eye contact can lead to a wellwishing or an argument. The pressure of all this will be much easier to bear if the candidate is an extroverted person. If a person likes to "recharge their batteries" by spending time alone, they may find the experience of being a candidate draining.

It should be kept in mind that the candidate and the message are inseparable. Any candidate for a cannabis law reform party must expect that people who do not know them well will refer to them as "the cannabis guy" or similar. A consequence is that the candidate will become a lightning rod for any prejudices about cannabis or about cannabis users. This must be seen as a good thing, because the stronger a person's prejudices against cannabis, the greater the potential to shift them towards a more enlightened position.

Attending Public Debates

If a cannabis law reform activist runs in an election, chances are good that they will be invited to a public debate with the other candidates. The activist must not let organisers of the debate restrict the candidates to those of the "established" parties. If this is attempted, the activist must fight to ensure that their voice is heard.

Any candidate from a cannabis law reform party will have a great chance of getting attention. The advantage with a multi-party debate is that it is less likely that a cannabis law reform activist will be attacked specifically on the cannabis issue, for the reason that the other parties will be arguing about the economy, education, defence and health. This means that a cannabis law reform candidate can practice a spiel that they can give in two or three minutes, and deliver it with little need for modification.

Because people have considerable prejudice against cannabis users, and because most people present already know what the conservatives, the social democrats and the greens are going to say, it is easy to come away victorious as a candidate for a cannabis law reform party. If an activist looks presentable, speaks coherently and presents an argument that appears, even on the face of it, to make sense, they will be the most surprising and therefore most memorable of all the options.

If you are nervous speaking in front of a crowd, the old psychologist's trick of imagining the audience naked really does work. Whether the activist is nervous or not, it can help to keep in mind that speaking in favour of a political platform in front of a crowd is something that few experience, so it ought to be savoured.

Get Your Story Straight

If a candidate uses a fact to support their argument, it is necessary that the fact be correct. There are two kinds of way that a fact can be correct, and they relate to the intellectual and the emotional methods of persuasion.

The intellectual side of the argument will be won if the facts accurately describe the reality of cannabis law reform. How much does it cost to keep a person in prison for a year and who supplied these figures? If the

229

candidate can answer both of these questions without pause they will demonstrate that they have an excellent grasp of the topic.

In some cases the candidate can share their reasoning with the audience ("one thousand cannabis prisoners at an hundred thousand dollars a year equals a hundred million dollars"). This is a great tactic because the audience are more likely to be persuaded if they feel that they arrived at the conclusions themselves rather than having been told.

The emotional side of the argument will be won if the candidates use the same facts. Little makes a party look less professional and trustworthy than contradictions in its own message or policy. It is best for the party to agree on the relevant facts before any serious media campaign - especially an election - is launched. This is where the role of the Information Officer becomes crucial - they are the one who must do the research, who must understand the facts and who must ensure that the rest of the party understands these facts.

Mailbombing

The closer the election is, the more justification the party has on spending money on media such as propaganda pamphlets. If the party has volunteer labour in a certain geographical area they can hit it with a mailbomb. This means that thousands of pamphlets are printed up and posted into every letterbox in a target area.

The best way to do this is to have three people and one car. One person drives the car full of pamphlets and the other two canvass either side of the street. If the campaign is large, care has to be taken not to hit the same letterboxes twice, and this will require a master map on which covered streets are marked with a highlighter.

One of the great things about mailbombing is that it is a logistical exercise that can be carried out at the branch level. Assuming that the party Information Officer has made propaganda pamphlets freely available on the party website, the branch representatives can download it, do a print run of it and then mail it. Because mailbombing requires three people it will give some activists an idea of the kind of cooperation that is necessary to succeed at any level.

Getting Out the Vote

Disappointingly, the supporters of cannabis law reform parties are amongst the least likely to actually vote. Surveys of disenchanted voters often reveal that a high proportion of them would have voted for cannabis law reform-friendly parties. Because it is also true that people who are not happy with the establishment as a whole (at least enough to question the value of voting) are more likely to be cannabis-friendly, a Get Out The Vote strategy is essential.

Several months out from an election, it might take hours of recruitment time to secure one new vote for the party. The day before the election, a twenty cent bulk text message might attract hundreds.

A rule of thumb that appears to hold true in multiparty

democracies is that a party gets fifty votes for every member it has. Another way of looking at this is that each member must seek to persuade fifty people to vote for the party. This is the calculus of the ground power half of the equation. Of course, air power will do some of the job, but it is best for activists to approach their work from the perspective that they need to persuade fifty people.

One way to ensure that a member draws fifty votes for the party is for them to make up a list of supporters and drive them to the polls. Many supporters of cannabis law reform will be too poor to have a car and will appreciate any help in getting to cast their vote. This is much easier to organise at the branch level, although the party website could help to arrange contact between those who can provide a lift and those who need one.

Another way is to enlist volunteers to call known members and supporters and cajole them into actually voting for the party on election day. If they have a problem getting to the poll booth, a message can be passed to whoever is responsible for driving people to the polls in that area.

Ideally, everyone who ever thought that voting for the Cannabis Party was a good idea should be reminded of this the day before the election itself. The party Membership Secretary can use their own membership lists to send messages as the election date approaches. These can be sent by email initially, although it is a good idea to send a bulk text message the day before the election with a very short call to arms.

That Final Moment

When people vote, sometimes they go into the booth knowing who their choice is and they go in and tick the box. If you can get supporters of cannabis law reform into this category, this is great. If not, it has to be hoped that the logo persuades them.

Whether a party logo attracts a vote is partially a function of how recognisable it is to the voter. This is why it is crucial to plaster it all over the party merchandise. Also for this reason it is a considerable gamble to use anything other than a cannabis leaf as a logo.

3. MISCELLANEOUS

Live As If It Were Legal

One of the best ways to fight for cannabis law reform is to live as if cannabis were legal. Ultimately, the choice to care about the legal status of cannabis is up to the individual. Cannabis can be smoked in the street if a person is willing to suffer the legal consequences of this.

The goal of this strategy is to normalise cannabis use in the public perception. Because cannabis is illegal, non-stoners do not encounter it often. For this reason, they will be impressed to see a person smoking cannabis in the street. If they see several dozen they might get a real shock, which might help them to understand just how many cannabis users there are out there (and how much it must be costing to conduct war against them all).

Key to this strategy is for the activist to behave as if smoking cannabis is no big deal. Explaining calmly and rationally that you do not consider cannabis use to be wrong will make a better impression than launching into a Martin Luther King style speech at someone who is just on their way to return some videos.

The Cannabis Closet

Like other lifestyles, an individual's openness to their own cannabis use can be described in terms of how far they are into the closet. The deeper, or more "in the closet" a person is, the less they admit to their cannabis use.

Deepest in the closet are the people who admit their cannabis use to no-one. Then come those who admit it to their closest confidantes, then those who admit it to their family, then those who admit it to anyone who asks (with the occasional strategic exception for police officers and the like). "Closet stoner" is a term given to a person who appears to be a stoner but does not admit to it.

Out of the closet is anyone who freely admits their cannabis use. Such people might even bristle at the use of the word "admit" for the reason that, because one admits to crime, it implies that cannabis use is a crime. Anyone making this argument is almost certainly out of the closet.

It is possible to come a long way out of the cannabis closet. Some cannabis users come so far out that their lifestyle is best described as "flamboyant." It is not difficult to understand the temptation to do this: it is a natural result of having been oppressed for so long. What is most important, from the perspective of a cannabis law reform activist, is what is best for the movement.

The Executive of the Party can and must use this as a measure of a member's loyalty and commitment to the cause. Writing a signed letter to a newspaper or standing for an election are two ways that a person can declare publicly, and therefore to anyone who knows them, that they are a supporter of cannabis law reform. Of course, neither of these is quite the same as a public declaration that a person is a cannabis user, but most people will make this assumption.

235

Any cannabis law reform activist must understand from the beginning that their status in the movement is heavily dependent on their relationship with the cannabis closet.

Displays of Solidarity

To get a proper cannabis law reform movement going, it is vital that the membership build up a sense of solidarity with each other. A gesture of solidarity will motivate everyone who partakes in it to do more for the cause. Sometimes the displays of solidarity are centred around an individual, and other times they are centred around the movement.

An example of the former case occurs when an activist is arrested and charged with a cannabis crime. Should that activist need to appear in court, the movement can create an impression by stacking the gallery with activists all wearing cannabis law reform t-shirts. If an activist gets let off a charge, those present will remember if it was cheered.

An example of the latter case is a spontaneous counterattack that is launched whenever the cannabis law reform movement is attacked in the media. If a politician comes out and speaks in favour of prohibition, they should be attacked along every line an attack can be made. Let the membership write letters to the editor of their local newspaper pointing out the reasoning errors or lies in the politician's statement (there will be some).

The core of solidarity is that if one of your members is abused, the abuser is attacked by all the other members.

Actually doing this will take some time to practice, but once it becomes instinctual, the movement will be preparing for victory.

The best example of the power of solidarity is the story of Spartacus. A slave mutiny was put down in Ancient Rome, and the Romans asked the slaves which of them was the Spartacus, the leader. It was clear that Spartacus was to be executed. All of the slaves claimed to be Spartacus themselves, and so shared his fate, whatever that should be. The cannabis law reform movement could achieve anything with this level of solidarity. It would mean that if one cannabis user got arrested in an area, thousands of other cannabis users would descend upon the police station and demand to all be arrested themselves.

Fighting in Court

Every dog has his day. The day of any given cannabis law reform activist could come when they are dragged to court for a cannabis offence. If a person does not believe in cannabis prohibition then the act of arresting and trying them is, to them, the true criminal offence.

The ultimate rejection of prohibition is to do a Roaring Lion. Refuse to acknowledge the authority of the court. Refuse to acknowledge the legality of cannabis prohibition. Refuse to acknowledge the sentence.

It is theoretically possible that if every person tried with a cannabis offence tried to drag the procedure out in the most costly manner, the court system would be overwhelmed by this and would be forced to throw the cases out owing to their low priority. This will remain a theory until everyone does it, but it is hard to take the opinion of anyone not in the court system seriously.

There is not enough space to give detailed instructions on how to beat a cannabis charge, but if an activist is aware of their rights and has access to a lawyer they will be better off than most.

Using Volunteer Labour

As the movement expands, the pool of volunteer labour hours available to the party will increase.

If there is no election on, the best use of volunteer labour hours is in increasing the pool of volunteer labour hours. This means signing up new members, and motivating current members to be more active.

If there is an election on, the best use of volunteer hours could be many different things, but helping candidates with their campaigns will be important at every stage. As election day draws near, all focus should be on the get out the vote campaign, which includes mailbombing and erecting billboards.

Community Outreach

There is no reason to limit the activity of a cannabis law reform movement to direct agitation for law reform. At all times the movement has a positive image to maintain, and a negative image to counter.

It should be kept in mind that a membership of a

thousand people is a considerable labour force if it were to be put to work. Even if a call for volunteers is put out and only five percent show up, if all of them are wearing a cannabis t-shirt this will create an impression.

Many people in the cannabis law reform movement will be skilled gardeners or landscapers, and if enough volunteers can be found this sort of work can be done as part of a fundraising effort. Failing this, a team of fifty workers doing even unskilled labour can raise hundreds of dollars an hour.

Public Submissions

In some cases, government or lawmakers will solicit public opinion before making a decision on a law. Of course, this never goes as far as necessarily doing what the people want, but it is still an opportunity for anyone to have their say on an issue.

If the government does ask for public submissions on a cannabis related issue, this is almost as exciting for a cannabis law reform movement as an election. It means the entire logistical machine can be thrown into action. For this reason it is an excellent idea to take public submissions seriously, as well as anything else that allows the party to work together. The election campaign will be much easier if the party has practised.

There is no need to limit the act of making a submission to the party. The party can make its submission, and every other member or supporter who also wishes to make one can do so. This lets people put the argument in their own words.

Slogans

These slogans are all short statements that can be written on a placard to take to marches or to protests. They are also valuable as signatures on internet forums. There are hundreds of possible slogans; here are only a few.

"Vote for us or go to prison."

Many cannabis users are blasé about who to vote for, reasoning that because all parties are made of politicians they must be equally crooked. Whether or not this is true, all but one of them wants to see cannabis users in prison.

"Cannabis use is not a crime."

This is an affirmation and a declaration of the rights of cannabis users.

"Good people do not recognise bad laws."

This explains why cannabis law reform activists continue to use cannabis despite it being against the law. The slogan is a retort to the idea that the law is the law and must be followed because it is the law.

"Grow the economy."

This slogan references the economic devastation wrought by cannabis prohibition, both on money wasted and potential earnings that are denied.

"Who am I hurting?"

This is to declare two things: cannabis use is a victimless crime and if an activity hurts no-one then no-one has the right to make it illegal.

"Dealers don't check for ID."

This refers to the fact that cannabis prohibition is worse for children than any kind of law reform, because the current system does little to keep cannabis out of the hands of youths.

"It didn't work for alcohol."

This points out that there is a historical precedent for law reform of drugs: alcohol prohibition was a failure, so we got rid of it.

The Single Convention on Narcotic Drugs

Even if a cannabis law reform movement can win the argument in both the media sphere and the ballot box, one ultimate problem remains. It is that almost every nation is a signatory to the United Nations Single Convention on Narcotic Drugs. This has had the effect of signing away the nation's sovereignty to the United Nations in the area of drug law reform.

Although it is theoretically possible for any nation to simply withdraw from the treaty, the prohibitionists will raise the spectre of international sanctions should this be suggested. There are, however, ways for cannabis law reform to succeed within the framework of the Single Convention.

One way is to keep cannabis illegal, as it is now, but ensure that both police and cannabis users are operating under an "understanding" that, as long as cannabis is used under certain conditions, police will not interfere. Which usually means: don't make a dick of yourself and it's all good. This is essentially the Dutch solution and will likely be close to the optimal solution short of withdrawing from the Convention.

Another is to restructure the police so that all drug enforcement activity must be funded from one specific account, which never has any money in it. This is an extreme form of deprioritisation - cannabis is still illegal but because there is no money to pay police to do anything about it the law cannot be enforced.

A third is to introduce a system of "strikes" under which people arrested for cannabis offences are given a number of warnings before any prosecution is made. The practical effect of this is similar to the first, because police are unwilling to do an hour of paperwork just to warn someone that if they do it several more times they might get a small fine.

Of course, the best way is to scrap the Single Convention altogether, which means that pressure must continue to be exerted upon politicians who may have some influence in this area. If a large number of countries voted cannabis law reform parties into power, even the most obstinate UN mandarin would have to concede that times have changed.

A Final Note I

At all times, the cannabis law reform movement must resist any and all efforts to divide it. There are not enough cannabis law reform activists to survive any kind of factionalisation, and prohibitionists are well aware of this.

The classic way of doing this is to set cannabis users who have different goals against each other. This has been used by prohibitionists in the USA to great effect. An example is when medical marijuana users achieve some rights, and then a proposal is made to grant rights to other cannabis users at the expense of medical marijuana patients. Do not fall for this - the division and infighting caused by such proposals do incalculable damage to the movement.

Another way of achieving this is to set cannabis users off against their natural allies. Alcohol was once prohibited, and many of the same wowsers responsible for that are responsible for cannabis prohibition. Likewise, many of the same people who believe that people should be free to drink alcohol believe that people should be free to use cannabis. For these reasons, the cannabis law reform activist should resist the temptation to attack alcohol and alcohol users, even if the evidence is clear that it does more damage to individuals and society than cannabis does or ever could. It is a strong argument to point out that if society can deal with alcohol it can deal with cannabis, but it is best to leave it at that.

Cannabis prohibitionists have been winning for close to a hundred years now, and this is because they are well funded and cunning. To turn the tide will, above all else, require that the cannabis law reform movement be at least as clever.

Never forget that you are fighting a human rights issue. As long as this is remembered you will have the enthusiasm to win.

A Final Note II

Do not compare prohibitionists to Hitler.